Like a Girl:
Perspectives on Feminine Identity

Dear Amy,

I hope you find the pieces
in this anthology to be inspiring,
heart-felt and, at times, amusing!
You're always danced to the beat
of your own drummer, and I think
that FABULOUS! :-) Warm regards,

Helen

Like a Girl:
Perspectives on
Feminine Identity

Edited by
Nancy Lynée Woo
Sarah Thursday
Terry Ann Wright

Copyright 2015 Lucid Moose Lit
Reprint permissions stay with the authors and artists.
ISBN-13: 978-0692486115
ISBN-10: 0692486119
Cover art by Rose Mary Neff
Layout and design by Sarah Thursday

Published September 26, 2015

The mission of Lucid Moose Lit is to stimulate conversation and foster community by publishing literature on social topics, while promoting literacy, creativity and diversity.

Social justice meets the arts.

Table of Contents

Mother

Sage

Acknowledgments

Introduction

Dear Readers,

The writing and art showcased between these covers respond to the question, *What is it to be "like a girl"?* One widely seen video from the company Always that aired in 2014 (#LikeAGirl) tackled this question. In it, girls of different ages are asked to demonstrate what it means to "run like a girl" and "throw like a girl." Young girls, 7 or 8, give a fierce demonstration of running and throwing, but teenage girls demonstrate with flimsy, feeble gestures that "like a girl" somehow came to mean for them: weak, pathetic, laughable. (Even as you read the word *feminine*, do you feel something negative bubble up?)

As women who used to be girls, the editors of this book were inspired to invite people to share their responses to the phrase "like a girl," and it has been a labor of love to showcase a selection of them in these pages. Though the views expressed here are not necessarily the views of the editors, we did take great care with our choices and hope you are as moved as we are by the compelling work included in this collection, which is, in its essence, an acknowledgment and a celebration of the broad spectrum of femininity.

What does feminine mean? Language is a fascinating construct, constantly changing; Merriam-Webster gives this definition: "Of, relating to, or suited to women or girls." We use the word "feminine" with intention to encompass a wide range of female, female-identified and genderqueer associations. The conversations could linger for hours, and we hope they do, about how language and experience interact with each other. We are not invested in perpetuating masculine/feminine binaries as a goal, necessarily, but in holding space for feminine experiences to be shared, and for complications to arise with respect and dignity. We honor all the voices bravely resonating in these pages, as well as those lying in wait.

As a press with a social justice platform, we think these are some important questions: When do girls learn society's expectations of them? Under constantly changing social pressure, how does any girl determine how to consciously exist in the world? How do women and female-identified individuals create a strong sense of self in any environment that, at best, simply may not understand them and, at worst, denigrates, abuses and mistreats them? Where do we find those precious moments of camaraderie and resilience? Who will tell our stories if not us? Who will appreciate them? How do we learn to thrive?

Any consideration of social identity is complex, and for every moment expressed between these covers, there are a million more out there; we hope this collection may present itself as a beginning or middle to a titillating conversation, and certainly not an end. What's missing? I hope perhaps you may create it.

I know I've been fortunate enough to read some wonderful coming-of-age novels (mostly in educational curriculum) about a young boy struggling into manhood. The literature has done its job: I feel close enough to these stories to empathize with that experience. Are growing boys lucky enough to say they have read enough literature about female coming-of-age experiences? Well, consider this a limited contribution to that end! We may not yet live in a world where every girl is inherently respected and celebrated for who she is and what she has to offer, with plenty of space for her unique voice to develop, but we as editors of this book would like to think we are doing our small part in helping to create that world. Every female experience is complicated and beautiful and messy and real, and worth many, many books. Yes, this is a feminist book. Yes, this is a book that recognizes a spectrum of gender and sexuality. And yes, we do hope that men, too, will take some time to explore these pages.

Maiden, Queen, Mother, Sage. From young girl to wise woman, feminine is a magnificent way to be in the world. While certainly fraught with challenges and pain, womanhood is as fascinating as it is complex. We gather in these pages moments of soul-lifting friendship and heartbreaking injustice, candid love and devastating betrayal, burgeoning sexuality and radiant body positivity, conflicted motherhood and powerful resilience. The voices presented here are vulnerable and strong, funny and dark, angry and gentle, fearful and joyous.

There are as many different ways of being feminine in this world as there are people, and every individual has her own unique experiences. But if there is one thing that feminine means to me personally it is this: we are strong when we come together. This anthology is a mosaic of voices, and we are so proud to share them with you.

Love and gratitude,
Nancy Lynée Woo
Editor-in-Chief

Maiden

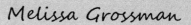

Melissa Grossman

Caught

Arms-over-head in a tangle,
taking off her flouncy dress,
her favorite – with a full, gathered skirt.

She is caught in the thought
that she is somewhere
between once and very soon.

The dress hangs from her hands,
like a theater curtain
between acts.

Jackie Joice
Girl in Pink Dress

Don Kingfisher Campbell

Kitty Hawk, California

Location: asphalt playground,
Garfield Elementary School, Alhambra
Starting Date & Time: 6 pm, Monday, April 26, 1999
Pilot: Kyla Campbell
Readiness: age 6, enthusiastic

DAY 1
Drove my nine-year-old red Nissan pickup to school
prospective pilot in shotgun seat
with pink bicycle featuring Barbie tassels
Walked bike to playground
pilot on seat
ready
Assisted pilot with takeoff
by holding on to back of seat
guiding, left hand lightly on handlebar
Flight!
Pilot gyrating wobbly half-circle and
as advised
stopping by
planting
landing gear
(both Barbie-sneakered feet)
Large ice cream smile
No falls, easy 45 minutes until sunset

DAY 2
Returned pilot and bike to playground
Today working on unassisted takeoffs
Right foot favored
for initial thrust
Pilot immediately swerved left
and recovered
Flight maintained in left-turning circles
Returned to home base one hour later

DAY 3
Tried sidewalk approach
Pilot extremely unsure of traveling
on narrow path in straight line
glancing fences
Aided steering with my ginger left hand
stabilizing seat
with gentle right
On playground pilot successfully
followed instructions
to create figure eights
Initiated sidewalk return
last 500 feet solo

Instructor now needs bicycle

Cat Dixon

Games

When I was a child, I played games
like war. We'd build dams made of pebbles
around puddles. Flood the ant hills.
Fleeing ants would be stomped or
carried to the fire with sticks.
My sister would call out as if she too
were an ant, "Please! Please don't hurt
my family!" Her high nasal
intimations seized us in giggles.
The mud clung to our white shoes.
A whole afternoon of murder.
When I was a child, I didn't notice
boys until the neighbor, blonde, blue-eyed
troll of eleven, asked to play on our front
steps. He tore off my favorite doll's head,
then raced to his bike
with her headless body. Her blonde head
discarded in my lap. I screeched.
I cried. Mother made me come inside.
The doll was never repaired, but I kept
the head in my treasure box under the bed.

Toti O'Brien
Citizen

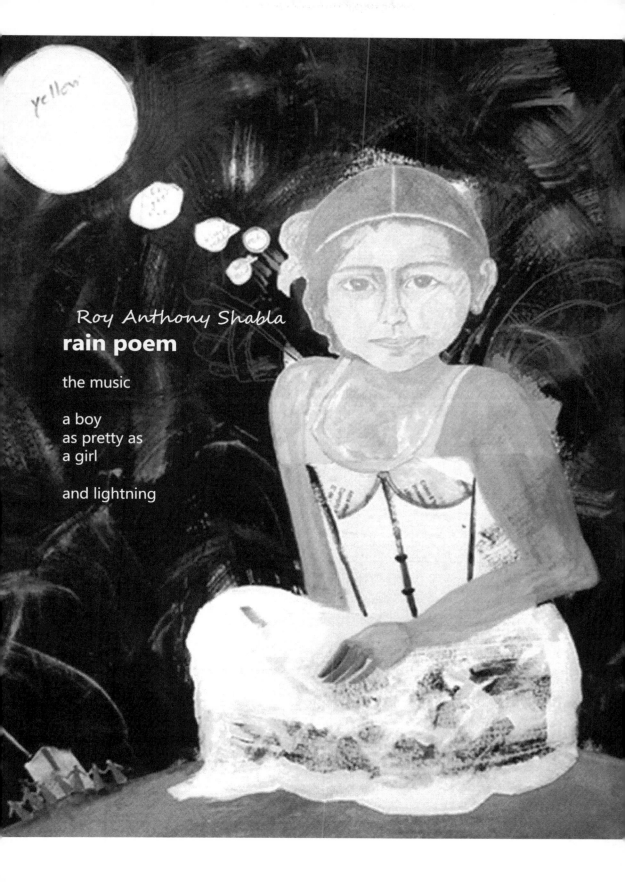

Roy Anthony Shabla

rain poem

the music

a boy
as pretty as
a girl

and lightning

Raundi Moore-Kondo

Sandbox Sweet-talk

It was sticky—all soft vowels
and spittle-laden consonants.
Lots of squeals and some spontaneous alliteration.
You sang songs about trains
and made jokes about your balls
that I only pretended to understand.

The way you burned-out on three wheels
told me that you were the kind of boy who rebelled
against bedtime rituals, green vegetables
and parental advisory warnings.

Despite one or two mild tantrums, I was wet riveted
by your helicopter and motorcycle impersonations.
You showed me how far cheesy goldfish could fly
and that boys are better than girls because they can pee
in bushes standing up without getting their socks wet.

Your devil-may-care juice box squeezes and roly-poly
autopsies both impressed and frightened me.
You enjoyed a little sand in my peanut butter sandwich
while explaining about your pet T-Rex.
No, you weren't scared—
He was trained and only ate girls.

You drove bulldozers and stolen police cars.
Ran Barbie down and buried her alive.
Then ate all the broken bits of sidewalk chalk
and made my last piece soggy sucking
on it like a cigarette.

The first time you called me "baby"
it was because I couldn't see smoke.

You got kinda quiet after skinning your knee.
Then yelled about hating jump ropes, your neighbor's
black dog with the spiked collar, and *babies,*
"Every God damned last one of 'em!"

You wished your dad wouldn't ever come home
and were especially suspicious of how big the bulge
in your mama's belly was getting.

I confided that blowing bubbles had become boring
both in swim class and in the bathtub.
I liked chocolate milk, frilly slips,
and the taste of pink Play-Doh best.

That's when you lifted my dress.
After seeing my panties, you dumped
out my Cheerios for the pigeons
and smeared boogers in my hair.

When your back was turned and you were in line
for the swings I hit you over the head
with your plastic-shovel.
God, how you cried.
I said something cute, like "Who's the baby now?"

Later that day after untying my laces
and right before shoving me backward
down the dark tunnel of the twisty slide,
you kissed me hard.

I can clearly recall the serrated edges
of both your bottom teeth and the first taste
of my own blood on someone else's lips.

Don Kingfisher Campbell

Fourth Lesson

inspired by Philip Booth's poem "First Lesson"

I was eyewitness to evolution last week.
This June my frightened intelligent daughter

avoided putting her head in the water.
She watched older, bigger people swim

and bobbed nervously with clamping hands
around the lip of the pool. Then

last week she visited her cousins,
saw kids her own size tadpole through

eyes open to the deep white concrete.
So Saturday she began to hold her nose,

close her mouth, put her face in to look
at the chlorinated world she stood in all summer.

On the fourth day Kyla discovered
the light nature of true buoyancy.

Her legs instinctively kicked, she moved
and was moved to find her body forward,

propelled to the other side of the wading square.
And back and forth she went, becoming

unafraid to fly under air, not wanting
to stop her newfound water-resistant motor

born on a September Tuesday:
girl swimming creature.

Amy Wright

The Little Little Little Little Little Little Dream

A dream is measured not by size
but what it does to a person, whether it turns

them another color on the inside, feels soft
as a mouse in the dark, tiny

squirming. Or hard. A book
with a wooden cover. Paper

thick as knives becoming solid
enough to knock on, open the door

of this small house constructed
from enough labor one might have fed

open mouths in a trailer
skillet-baked, hand-churned buttered

cornbread, the way her mother did,
wanting only to be a mother.

The only Rome apple
in the grocer's bin she reached her white

hand into, found its crisp walls dusky
with orchard freckles—stars on a plain night

in a plain town that served no woman
but a girl whose people called her becoming

when her panties spotted, meaning now
her promise could begin to be exhausted.

She could look down on
herself—sweated up, having run

all this way for nothing to grandma,
who would be on the back porch all afternoon.

Melissa Grossman

Her Secret

The word *crusty* made her cringe.
Not because it reminds her
    of well-baked bread,
Not because it makes her think
    of the clown on The Simpsons.
And not because she hates
        the dried residue of sleep that collects
            in the corners of her eyes.

It is *that* word her mother used
    to describe her most personal,
        most private part of her little girl body.
It is why her mother needed to scrape her clean.

Fernando Gallegos
She kept the music to herself

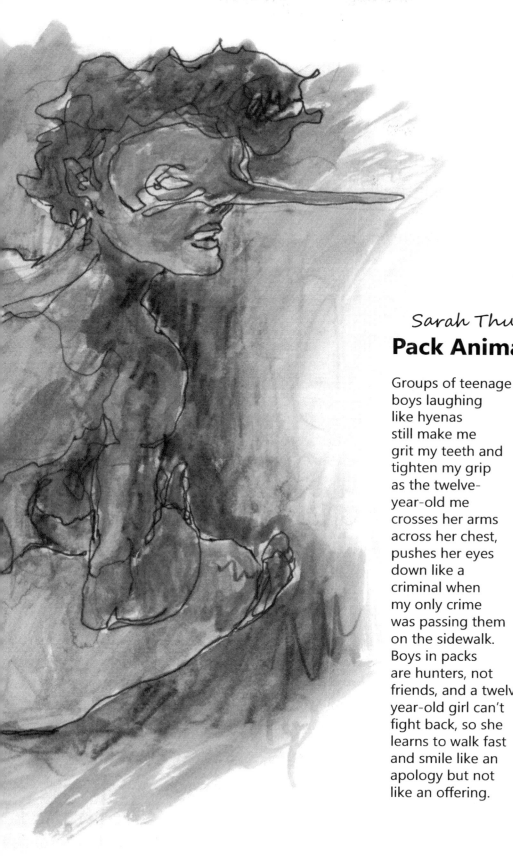

Sarah Thursday

Pack Animals

Groups of teenage
boys laughing
like hyenas
still make me
grit my teeth and
tighten my grip
as the twelve-
year-old me
crosses her arms
across her chest,
pushes her eyes
down like a
criminal when
my only crime
was passing them
on the sidewalk.
Boys in packs
are hunters, not
friends, and a twelve-
year-old girl can't
fight back, so she
learns to walk fast
and smile like an
apology but not
like an offering.

Jennifer Jackson Berry

When I Was a Girl

doctor visit was: pride during my pre-6th grade physical when
she parted my lips & apologized for pulling some hairs.
i was soon for a full bush. hairless was for everywhere but

down there. i pressed the electric razor against my shins, but
no reason to press so hard it cut me. i shaved my arms when
the wisps were like so many question marks, *why so much hair?*

why aren't you normal normal normal? i hated (not pubic) hair
with the same heat i loved my new body (breasts!) but
when the doctor frowned, then suggested a 1,200 calorie diet, when

she didn't want to celebrate my hair, but instead reduce
my body, that was when
everything started to change

When I was a girl

treasure was: bop, teen beat, tiger beat, posters of the two
coreys before drugs & death, kirk cameron, ralph macchio, school
books wrapped in brown grocery bags with penciled graffiti & bubble

letters 2 good 2 be 4 gotten from best friends, bubble
gum shared piece by piece, split heart necklaces worn on two
necks, id bracelets with a boy's name for the lucky ones, school

field trips to the aviary & plays & museums, back-to-school
shopping for erasers stickers scented markers bubble-
wrapped trapper keepers & pop-a-point pencils. no more trips to

the back of the school-room to sharpen, to imagine the word bubbles
above the heads of the bullies: *fatso!*

When I was a girl

fashion was: anything slimming, vertical stripes, black, but
nothing exactly like a skinny girl's because of the inevitable
comparisons. puffy paint, jackets laced with novelty pins,

pegged jeans, jeans pegged tight with a safety pin
so no bending over to fix the cuffs & showing my butt,
then sports team shirts, british knights, bugle boy & inevitable

androgyny of same. baggy & boyish inevitably
hid what everyone else showed. the anti-pin-
-up. & just in case, sweaters long enough to cover my butt.

fashion makes the woman, but inevitably girls like me are pinned,
stuck between butch & a soft place

When I was a girl

all day   i dream   about sex
i dream   about all day sex all day
i day dream   about sex all

day i dream sex   about all
all about   day i dream sex
all day i dream about sex all day

i dream about sex all day
all day   i dream all about sex all
about sex   all day i dream

dream day   i   all about sex

Meg Eden

Schürze

Mother shows me the aprons she salvaged
in the bottom hall closet—the flour sacks
converted, X-stitched monograms,
a woman's lineage—through the fabric,
I almost hear the silenced voices
of these women before us.

Mother unfolds an apron she bought from Germany
right before marrying my father. "I was so excited
to be a home *frau*," she says. She unfolds a smaller
one, the apron I wore as a child, lace made
from old curtains. She places it on top of the stack.
"I will save these for your marriage,
for your daughters," she says.

I think of the women that have told me,
*I always wanted to write a book. I wanted to travel,
but I never did. Life catches up to you.* I think
of the mothers of Japan, settling into greying
cement depression, their husbands in love hotels.

I think of wearing an apron and equating this
to my only happiness. I want to shout, *Is this it?
Is this the reward for our labors?* Mother tells me,
There are seasons with different priorities.

I try to imagine my older body, buried
wearing this crown of womanhood.
Will my voice, too, be trapped in the fabric
so that the girls to come press their ears to the apron,
listening for my laundry list of endured hardships—

I run the fabric through my fingers and hide
them from my child-eyes.
I do not tell her, but I am afraid.

Toti O'Brien

Myself as the Iron Girl

Alexis Rhone Fancher
Zöe's Perch

JL Martindale

The poem about the straight girl who decided I needed a coming out intervention after she kissed me first

She painted her nails with Wite-Out
carving skulls, hearts by ballpoint
claimed she liked my apocalyptic poetry
and Sharpied epics down my leg.
Gutted men and pierced appendages
bled black through my blue jeans,
down our naked thighs.
She injected love letters in red-inked Bic
over my neck and shoulders
during duPratt's lecture on the gilded age
where pretty girls' affections destroy
only men.

Cat Dixon

Red Carnations

the corsages are   floating angels   in the park fountain
high school prom groups   snap photographs   before the dance
he loiters   the boutonnieres flap   in the wind
the wrapped stems
pinned. pin
through and under the stem at an angle.
later he rakes all of me into a collection for the keeping
like a disturbing display of butterflies pinned to a board
for a school science project. i protest
this intense examination.

discord grows after the fireworks show—it's midnight
walking to the car from the stadium. after he chases me, pins me to the street
and demands i listen, we go to his house. he bandages my skinned knee,
says he will buy me a new shirt, and wants to make love.
raw edges line buttonholes to
prevent fabric fraying. i cannot go home.
i cannot sew. all summer i wear long sleeves.

Karen Boussioneault-Gauthier

The Flower

Donna Hilbert

The Swimmer

Brown hair stuffed in a cap
strapped under my chin, I swam
through junior high summers
at the Reseda Park pool,
in water heavy with chlorine.
All summer I smelled
like the sink
Mother sprinkled with Comet
before leaving for work.

Maxine's mom was a dry cleaner.
Days off, she cadged
invitations to swim
in backyard pools of the rich
whose clothes she pressed,
steamed in her shop.
Mother said she was nervy
just like Maxine. Like Maxine,
her hair was curly, dark.

Days after swimming,
we dipped crackers
in mustard, Worcestershire,
any liquid found in their kitchen
went into our sauce,
an extra-strength potion.
We dipped, ate, were transformed
into amazing girls:
scientists, swimmers.

At school in September:
Whose tan is darkest?
Which camp is better,
Malibu, Pine Flats?
I longed to be one of *them*
a Valerie or Susan,
whose long blonde hair
turns green every summer.

Daniel McGinn

Beautiful Girls in Swimsuits

Beth Cooley

Facts of Life

The birds and the bees was not a term we used in our house. We had no euphemism for reproduction, no codename for sex. Instead we didn't mention it at all. Though inarticulate, we weren't totally in the dark; pregnant ladies appeared at church, teachers disappeared from school before they began to show. Babies were born, and we knew storks didn't deliver. Our parents slept in the same double beds in the same master bedrooms in houses all over town. But what they did in those beds was never talked about. We had no word for *pleasure*.

Still, the unnamed facts remained, so when I turned twelve I came home from school to find a box on my bed. It was about the size of a Kleenex box but square. I remember the design, pink and orange circles blending into each other like Venn diagrams. Very groovy. Although the swinging 'sixties had detoured around Laurinburg, NC, we recognized the trappings. The box probably sported a slogan written in prim cursive across the top. Maybe "A Gift for You!" which was a dead giveaway, code for not-a-real-gift-but-something-someone-thinks-you-should-have. I picked up the box and shook it.

I suppose the box really was a gift, though my mother didn't actually place it in my hands. She wasn't even in the room when I opened it with some trepidation, remembering the print of Pandora that hung in the school library. I rummaged through the contents: a booklet printed in apologetic pastels, a puffy Kotex that I could not imagine wearing between my legs, an even more unimaginable Tampax in a hard cardboard tube, and a plastic case covered in psychedelic squiggles. The squiggles were meant to assure me this whole experience was somehow cool. But I knew better. This was The Curse, The Little Friend. Periods. Or *menses*, as the booklet put it, introducing one of several new words hidden like bedbugs in the pastel pages.

"Let me know if you want to talk about anything after you read the literature." My mother's voice snuck up behind me. The Tampax jumped from my hand. She must have been hovering outside my bedroom door. Waiting for me to discover the box sitting in the middle of my bed. Her smile flashed bright and fearful. Then she closed the door.

After you read the Literature. The word sounded strange coming from my mother. This wasn't literature, it was an instruction manual/life sentence/insincere apology thinly veiling the shame and inconvenience of becoming A Woman. I turned the pages with growing gloom.

Small-town North Carolina circa 1970 was neither the time nor the place for celebrating a young woman's puberty. At around twelve years old, boys went hunting or deep sea fishing. As far as I know, no one talked about this event in terms of rites of passage or blood rituals; still the boys got to kill something and bring it home, a buck or a duck or at least a fish. But girls— we got to shave our legs the Easter we turned thirteen. This was a blood ritual in its own right, since most of us nicked the hell out of our shins and still have the scars to prove it. It was much later that I heard about initiation gifts, ritual ear piercings with 18K gold studs, special lunches with aunts and godmothers (no one I knew even *had* a godmother). Even in my twenties I had a hard time imagining the hugs and happy tears shed by mothers more enlightened or less inhibited than mine, who would have found any celebration of biological function (outside a tasteful baby shower) highly inappropriate.

When I started my period the summer after The Box, I was at Camp Skyuka in the Appalachian Mountains bunking in a cabin with nine other girls. The crusty brown stuff I found on my cotton underpants one morning puzzled me until I realized what it was. Then I was so terrified I could hardly make it out of the bathroom without passing out. When I did, I told my camp counselor what I needed, whispering the word. *Kotex*. What? *Kotex*. She looked puzzled and I repeated it again, louder. Then her face broke into blushing surprise. Her name was Kitsey. She was the sweet counselor, and she kept asking how I felt. Fine, fine. I felt fine. I also felt lucky that I didn't have Iris for a counselor. Iris was the big-mouth. Iris would have told. So, things could have been worse. Still I couldn't swim for a week. I remember sitting by the cool mountain lake in shorts and a tee-shirt sweating, swatting horseflies, with a thick bandage strapped between my legs.

What I don't remember is whether I called my mother to tell her what had happened. Phone calls were only for emergencies. Was this an emergency? I can't imagine that I wrote the facts out in words in a letter. Maybe I waited until I got home, abundantly grateful I had been away when it happened. Eternally thankful I had been alone.

But back to The Box. After I read the pastel pages in all their clinical acuity, after I studied the highly technical diagrams of *vagina, uterus* and *ovary,* testing the new words in my mouth, mispronouncing each one, I put everything back in the box. I lay on my bed until the mild nausea passed. Then I put the box on my closet shelf with other stuff I didn't really need and waited for my mother to tap softly on my door.

"Do you have any questions?" If there was ever a sentence designed to kill all further inquiry, this is it. I shook my head.

"Fine. Just let me know." As she closed my bedroom door for the second time that afternoon, I read relief in her eyes. And something else, something I didn't have a word for then. Now I call it pity.

Danielle Mitchell

What I Mean
When I Say Cartwheel

The skinny girls could
kiss their hands to the crow-eaten field
swivel their hips, legs sailing through the air
like the propeller of an I'm-not-sorry engine,
but I couldn't. Said, must be too tall,
would rather stand here & shit talk
pull hair, hold you by the arms & spin
& spin until our worthless bodies
sank to the pocked grass. I am always
out of breath or about to inhale
on a constricted sternum, which is to say
angry. Bigger than the boys.
Relying on the meanness of friends
to surpass the cruelty of the older girls who
all my life took pride in setting my hair
on fire, filling my mouth with worms.
I mean absent, I mean sick.
The school yard scaling over with
a summer heat that wouldn't quit, all of us
hanging by our knees in the moon
climb & I mean sucking it in,
waiting it out. Prayer for the hip-sway,
may it fall into all the right places.

Elena Rodriguez

Echoes of Mine

Donna Hilbert

Vocabulary Builders

Like pieces of fruit
exposed to radiation
they grew
the summer I turned thirteen.

AA to DD in just three months!

That September I was queen
of the girls' locker room.
Even the rich girls in lace
panty and bra sets
quit being mean.

Boys talked about me now
and I overheard:

breasts boobs knockers
hooters honkers zonkers tits
mammeries zobies lungs

My vocabulary grew
like an infestation of fruit flies—
nothing could stop it.

Melissa Grossman

Fat Girl

I carry the weight of being a fat girl.
I bear the indelible sledgehammer taunts:
      my brothers calling me "tank"
      people saying "how beautiful" I'd be if I "just lost weight."
I wear the weight like battle armor, hiding my anger.

I carry the raw egg of my future on a spoon.

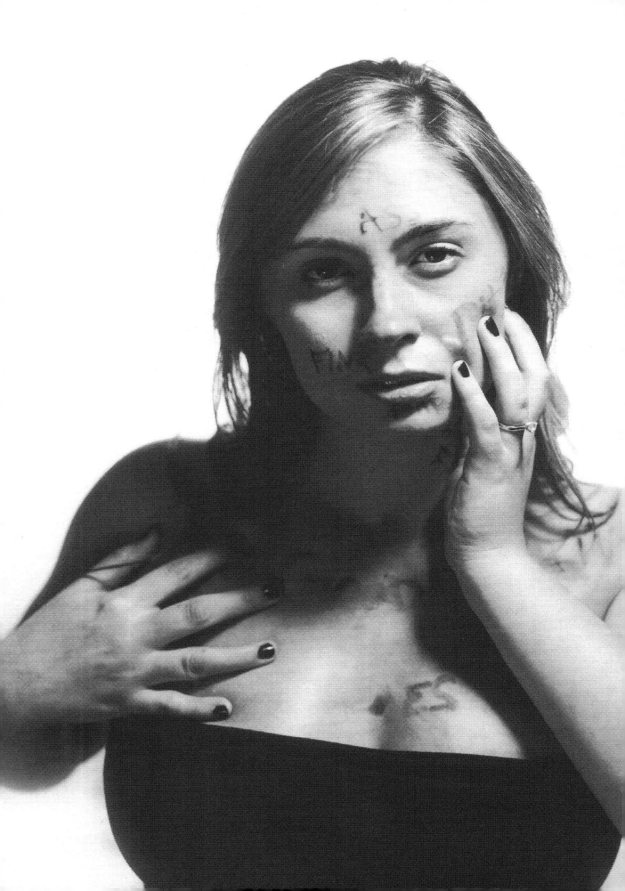

Beth McIlvaine

Shedding

There are days when I would crush the girl out of me
if I could.
I would take my thumbs to the clay of my hips
and push the swell flat.
I would crumple my hair into a quick and bloody twist
of scalp.
I would eat myself down to the gristle
and the marrow
and I would eat that too.
Salt and stipple of my fat, bitter organ,
all those heavy tides,
some days I would trade every secret
for another secret.
I would trade this open throat
for a ringing bell.
I would unlovely, unround, unbecome
this tender, this joy,
this folded prayer.
I would prune myself down to
boy-stone
and feed him fingers of myth.
We would burn down
our heart
like a sugar cane field.
Even now, we are watching the ash rise
our belly full of dumb,
screaming blood.

Chelsea Krob
Strip

Alison Stone

Men Want the Blonds,

but marry the brunettes, my father announces
as I lie on the deck in my new bikini, Sun-In
bleaching streaks in amber hair.
My dark-tressed mother's in the kitchen
in a one-piece, putting bologna on bread.
36-26-36 is ideal, he continues,
strolling by with the mail—Playboy
and bills—*but 24-34-24 is cute, too.*
Do I measure up? Later I hold string around my chest,
trying to understand the looks
boys give me, why the doctor's fingers
linger, the tone in my father's voice
that makes me want to disappear.
I keep a sweater in my school desk
and wear it no matter the weather, desperate to camouflage
these mounds that seem to have sprouted overnight,
requiring a C cup with straps
that groove my shoulders, while the other
fourth-grade girls wear undershirts or soft training bras.
It happened early to me, too, Mom commiserates.
I hunched my shoulders to hide.
Taller than my teacher,
with hips that slow running, I have to bring
my birth certificate to movies to pay the under-twelve price.

A child with a woman's shape
is still a child, and what kid
doesn't want power? The way boys stare
and nudge each other thrills me,
even as it makes me more alone.
My flat friends thrust their chests out,
sing, *We must, we must,*
we must increase our bust. Their giggles a wall
between us. Not sure what to do
with my new body, I hope
Dad's magazine girls can help. I sneak
Playboy from his bathroom and stare.

They stare back, long legs spread, pubic hair
a perfect triangle, eyes wide
in stupor or surprise. Their breasts are bigger than mine,
small planets, nipples impossibly pink.
What are their glossy mouths trying to say?
I want their secrets,
want to wear a sailor hat and bend over
the deck of a yacht, or place one fishnet-clad
leg on the railing, a tall drink in my hand.
I don't want to be brunette and angry, fighting with my husband
about "headaches," always washing pots.
I will be this other kind, made-up and desired,
shiny as a doll. I have no idea
where I'm going or how to get there, but I trust
my gold hair will light the way.

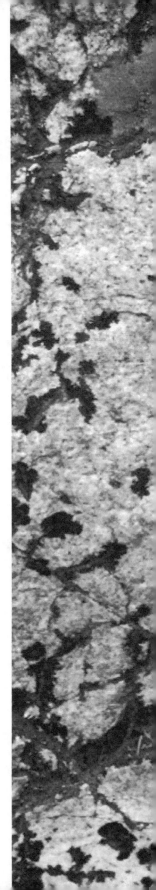

JL Martindale

When they told me
I would not be assigned Sylvia Plath

They blamed my red to black crust bracelets
glass carved over three days, just deep enough
to earn a seventy-two hour involuntary stay
in Van Nuys.
For my own good, they said,
shoe laces and necklaces were confiscated
while pale-faced wide-eyes peeked
from yellow-lit hallway of cracked doors,
pajama'd teens glaring at the new girl,
sizing me up, judging my damage on the swell
of my eyes and cheeks, tear chapped.
They could not read my bandages
hidden beneath the baggy green hoodie
I never went without. Not even in summer.
Choosing to live-hide inside my own personal oven
rabbit-trap-snare, swearing ich ich ich-k,
I'd grow up, learn my way out of hospitals
by taking love like barbed wire.
No daddy told us we deserved better.

Debbie J Cho

Hand

Don Kingfisher Campbell

The Artist

draws in my notebook
hers has been full for 20 minutes

she draws the same things
the same scene over and over

Mom, Dad, Kyla, all with smiling faces
standing next to a house
(we live in an apartment)

the sun is in the upper left hand sky
radiating hairy-looking lines above our heads

clouds float like barbeque smoke
over the windows I taught her to cross

with the sign of God—four panes
eyes to the empty residence

we're always outside—like real life
off to school, swim, McDonald's,

the beauty demonstration, the rare family
poetry reading; and when it's dark, home

for a video, a bedtime book; when it's
not too late—when I'm not mad

that she didn't put away her toys,
clothes, hangers—I try to teach her

without ever hitting or yelling
because I did that once

she took the smile off my face
on the next day's drawing

I never want to cry like that again

Tamara Madison

Drawer

A few days after the seduction
he decides to talk to me,
asks me to go to the clinic.
Make sure there is no growth,
he says.

Now I am looking up at the light.
My knees are spread and two women
sit at the foot of my table.
They carry on a lively conversation
as they work. I'm not listening.
I feel the warm light
on my newly-wakened
nether world,
and the women begin
to search inside me
as in a drawer.

I imagine them pulling things out –
bottle caps, old tires, tampons of course,
lipstick tubes, wrappers, leaves,
a shred from *Seventeen* magazine...
But I'm not so old, I want to protest,
I've barely begun my collection!

You're fine, they tell me
and hand me a prescription
to make me bleed. Outside
it's raining. I sit in French class
staring out at the rows
of eucalyptus dripping
in their ragged bark,
at the stream of bicycles
hissing on the wet path.
I watch him round the corner
as always at this time,
beard trimmed,
carrying his violin,
too old to be a student.

Susan Lefler

Iraqi Shadow Box

Her small feet pick a path
through rubble. Palms
line the street. A bomb
has scrambled pavement.
Hair pulled back from her face,
she wears a hand-smocked dress
and clutches something dark
beneath her arm. A cat? A coat?
She stares ahead. Her shadow falls
across the torn street,
circles her ankles, threatens
to pull her down.

Claire Ibarra
Dayglow

K. Andrew Turner

Sharcas

Grandpa calls me a silly girl
when I watch the sun set.
I love the vibrant hues,
the transformation
from orange
       to red
           and purple
the painted vaults of the sky.

I watch the Gods lower the sun
and leach the vivid color
into homogenous, inky black.
Only pinpricks of light
that we call sharcas—
wandering flames.
I wish to wander with them,
dance in the velvet blanket,
but Grandpa calls me silly.

I am supposed to be strong
support our village
      by feeding them
      protecting them
I am told I should be
like my brother.

But all I want to do
is gaze into the ether
and leave these chains behind
and soar with the sharcas
forever free
forever free
no longer a silly girl
but a woman
burning bright
shedding hope in
eternal darkness.

Daniel McGinn

Dad with Mystery Woman

Alexis Rhone Fancher

Under Water

Forget them. The men who looked right through you, used you up,
the ones you opened wide for when you should have run.
Forget about pop songs you listened to in secret, ones that made you
think someone was out there, just for you. It isn't true.
Forget the fumblers, the degenerates, the bad boys, the all-that-you-deserves.
That fast-talking charmer who popped your cherry in the dark?
The baller who refused to give you head? The rich kid who left you at
the hotel, holding the bill? All bastards, still.
Don't line up all those New Year's Eves when everyone else was a couple.
That line will conga out the door. Nothing comes easy. Nothing goes right.
You swear it builds character, or some Nietzsche shit.
You don't sleep at night.

You deserve to rut in those desperate times, daddy's bourbon in your glass,
mama's Vicodin in your pocket, those B-movie plots in your head.
Given the choice, you'll always go with the angrier option,
the one that guarantees pain. Admit it! You're a sucker for drama. It's tattooed
across your forehead, neon-lit behind your eyes.
You've gone over it a million times and still you're none the wiser.
So do yourself a favor. Forget trust. Forget love. Forget your goddam dreams.
Forget your happy childhood, the ponies, the neglect. Forget your straight A's,
your perfect pitch, your mastery of all things French.
Forget about having a normal life; it's all rubbed out, erased,
because you can't forget the pool man who grabbed you in the deep end,
who stripped you, squeezed you till you cried, till you let him touch you,
till you let him finger you, till you admitted it felt good.

40

Terry Wolverton

Little Mermaid

Blood on the moon scares me
but I don't want the mermaid's cure.

Listen. I am only eight
when the world dissolves.

Doctor rocks me to sleep until
everything is taken away.

I tongue the near-deaf darkness;
I open to no one.

Mermaid can't find her way
back to the sea. Was it worth it?

I take the scalpel between my thighs
though I bite only the world.

Ashley M. Jones

spin•ster

noun \'spin(t)-stər\

1. a woman whose occupation is to spin

I am caught in a revolving door. This is unlike the princess at the wheel, waiting for Rumplestiltskin's tinny laugh and pecking eyes. The days just keep seeping out of the calendar's mouth like phlegm. I have not felt the bristle of moustache hair in years. I would spin it into the finest cloth.

2. *archaic* : an unmarried woman of gentle family

My mother got married when she was twenty-seven. She met my father in college—that's how it's done. That's when nice young boys and nice young girls converge. In Alabama, the least you can do is meet a nice co-ed when you're swimming knee-deep in them. In Alabama, marriage is the next step—high school, college, marriage. Then career. If career. Then kids. Always kids.

3. a woman who seems unlikely to marry

When I was ten, I chose the boy with the unibrow who wore a pleather jacket in the springtime. I didn't wear lip gloss because it felt like vap-o-rub. I didn't wear skirts because my legs were too skinny. He walked with me, let his arm touch mine, let his eyebrow ripple with intrigue when I walked his way. This was it.

But no boy likes to be put in a corner. No boy likes to be owned.

He said he hated me and took another girl to the dance the next week.

F. Douglas Brown

Dear Defiance

As your daddy I shouldn't say this but
One day I want you to stand up
To your brother and if need be, punch him
In the face or last resort, the ding-ding,
Defying all little girl rules
Of etiquette and grace.

In fact, I want you to have your girliest-
Girl stuff on when this moment manifests.
I want his friends present, their eyes wide
As whale mouths, witnessing defiance,
A surge of feminine power sparking
Across your brother's head.

I imagine gravity letting you lift off
I imagine smooth hands
Connecting to smooth chin.

I imagine a short scuffle thereafter, and
Your eyes not pulling off or down:
Poised brows, the unyielding
Blush on your cheeks.
The grit. The sweat.

But right now, your sobby speech is a wet
Newspaper smearing into my shirt.
Your tears move down fast, as
Fast as a brother's wicked
Ways, fast as the future
Of your left hook.

Christine Brandel

The Summer No One Told Us Would Change Our Lives

We pushed our hands in soft, damp dirt to pull the bodies of the plants out of the ground. We were in love with the lilies of the valley, the fallopian curve of their stems and the delicate whiteness of their bells. We wanted to take them with us though we left them in the sun when we entered the barn and I misjudged the safety of the hay which did not hold me like a mother should after I jumped into the air.

You carried me into the home and put me into a warm tub until I followed you into the bedroom. You said, your body is broken now, it's unlikely you'll walk again. I knew this to be untrue as I had carried my own self into the room and had placed my own body next to yours on the mattress. You leaned over and wiped your whistle against my wet hair. You teased your hand into my mouth and took my tongue, secreting it in your pocket like a watch. Turning me over, your fingers drew the line of my spine until you located the bone you wanted as your own and it joined my tongue in your pocket. I have hips, I said and you said, I know.

Take your tablets, you told me, tossing me a bottle of pills. They were pink. As you left I found your face becoming.

Outside night had fallen, like I had, but its blackness was filled with bicentennial fireworks that dropped like drizzle from the sky. I imagined little white flowers falling into your hair. I imagined your voice singing like the ringing of bells that told children they were too late. I swallowed your medicine. My body was never the same.

Daryna Barykina

Stigma

Queen

Yvonne M. Estrada

Eastbound to Tempe

60 freeway horizon,
black divided road,
we wheeze through diesel,
pinch our noses,
pass fragrant dairy farms,
windows down, June drizzle flies in,
scent of wet asphalt
mingles with dead freeway grass.
Semi's monstrous rumbles,
piercing squeaks between double trailers,
truckers look down at our girl legs,
trumpet air horn,
their tongues and words whip back
and away like straw wrappers.
In this split second we treat them
as if they even exist in our world,
screaming, laughing, waving.

Helen Yeoman

Fabulous

Dear Victoria,

Today, I received your recent brochure advertising your newest collection: FABULOUS. According to you, Fabulous is approximately 5'11" and 118 pounds. Fabulous sports a natural-looking, fake tan and beachy Bardot waves. She wears matching Barbie pink bra and panty sets while cuddling with puppies. As my two-year-old nephew would say, *Aaaaahhhhh, cuuuuute!*

On the next page, Fabulous dons a sophisticated ivory and black lace strapless bra, again with matching panties, and completes the look with black pumps. She kneels on her bed, pretending to eat huge slices of cake and pastel macarons.

In the evening, Fabulous slips into her rhinestone-encrusted navy pushup and matching thong. Sparkling like a star, she spends hours in her shoe closet laughing as she tries on pair after pair of stilettos, apparently the only style of shoe she owns.

Really, Vicky? I agree with you that "Life is Fabulous!" But I've created my own brochure, and it looks something like this...

Puppy? Sure, I love puppies. But we're in a park, and I'm fully clothed in sweats. My Bardot tresses have instead been swept into a greasy ponytail because I've been (don't die of shock) sweating. Hold on V, cuz it's about to get worse.

Flip the page, and you will see me actually *eating* both the cake and macarons. As a former dancer, I realize that's it's possible to survive on nothing more than an apple, spoonful of cottage cheese and cocaine; however, it's not a diet that ever enticed me nor one I'd recommend to others. Therefore, I'm approximately 140 pounds. I'm dressed in my favorite comfy tee from summer camp 1989. My shirt is older than Miss Fabulous. My bras and panties rarely match. I've discovered my breasts and waist shrink and expand at approximately the same rate. I've yet to confirm exactly how Fabulous maintains her C or D cup size while keeping her flat abs since I'm forced to choose between the two. Based on my years of experience working for both fitness and men's magazines, I'm pretty sure Fabulous achieves her glowing looks with some combination of the following formula:

Chelsea Krob

Everywhere

compulsive exercise + photogenic genetics + starvation + surgery + makeup + lighting + Photoshop (a gal's best friend) = somebody's standard of "beauty."

On the back of my brochure, my closet is spilling over with piles of unread magazines, spiral notebooks, clothing hangers and yes, boxes of shoes, but only a few containing stilettos. Two large cartons are stuffed with cards sent from people I've cherished for years before you started mailing me your ridiculous brochures.

So as I toss the coupon you lovingly included into the trash, I'll fill you in on my secret: At thirty-eight, I've figured out when someone is trying to sell me something and when what they have to offer isn't as grand as what I already possess. I know the price others have paid, seen the scars stretching across their breasts before their photos have been retouched. Fabulous, I see, is a fantasy. Even her life is too skinny, which is why it fits into a small, ten-page brochure.

My life, by contrast, is fleshier, overwhelming, both full and fulfilling, decadent...and it tastes fabulous!

No longer yours,

Helen

Sheila Cooper

Solidarity

Girl, please.
Your blues ain't mine.
All this time you keep trying
to make me you,
deny me my Black and Blue.
Child, please.
You need to recognize:
your blues ain't mine.

Honey, stop.
Your blues ain't mine.
All this time I keep trying
to be me,
while you try to whitewash me
into an image of you.
Stop, boo.
Your blues ain't mine.

I know you want to hold hands
and shout that your struggle is mine
Well, okay, bless that.
That's cool. That's fine.
But before we can ever seek
out some kind of solidarity,
I need you to look at me
and really see.

Before you can even imagine
what it feels like being
Black me,
you need to look at me.
You need to see me,
not what you perceive me to be.

So, blessed sister,
I know you love me,
and down the line,
True that: our struggle
is intertwined.
But before we can reach solidarity,
I need you to see me,
and realize:
your blues, just ain't like mine.

Lee Kottner

What I've Learned From Men

From my father, fixer of gooney birds:

not to cut the lawn barefoot; to keep
knives and saws sharp and
shoes shined; know
the uses of *grimple* and how to
pack for any occasion; when
to ask for a parachute; to always
get back on the horse, show 'em
who's boss, plan
for contingencies, pay attention to
the wind chill, get out of bed if necessary
to see the aurora, be early,
check the exits, and
find the North Star.

From my grandfather in his fedora:

how to make a neat stack of dimes, eat a
rare T-Bone, see beauty in neon and
Wurlitzers; how to prime a pump, and
how much a jigger is; to play cribbage,
tap my fingers, tie my shoes, blow bubbles;
to find pleasure in writing at a fine desk
with a fountain pen, in driving fast,
in superballs and jacks, in ants and bottle
caps and kitsch.

From various uncles, living and dead:

to bait my own hook, play at least two
moves ahead, and break in a baseball mitt;
to know what to throw back, take good
black and white photos and love pick-up trucks;
have the patience of fishermen; how to
miter a corner, and develop a relationship
with Siamese cats.

From past lovers, insignificant things:

how to hold a hammer and when
to let go; to tell Handel from Mozart,
beer from ale, lust from passion, yes
from *no* but not *maybe*.

What I learned from the rest:

how to choke an engine to life; to
lean precipitously on curves; when
to go over the top and when to slide,
how to back up and when (never) to
back down; how to bluff and when to
call; how to be one of them

and not myself.

Denise R. Weuve

Dear Stepmother,

I am tired of picking
lentil beans from the fiery
ash just to doll-up
in a ball gown
that is too much taffeta,
too much pink.
What good anyhow?
My feet are callused,
burns scar my fingertips,
and my lungs are filled
with household disinfectant.
Let your daughters and their
caustic tongues lead them to the castle
and that tidy Prince Charming.
I wipe my hands clean
in this feeble apron,
call it a day.

See, even if I did not mind
the glass slippers
cutting into the flesh
above the toes,
as I pirouetted to a man's lead,
I have met the baker
two villages east.
He has oven-warm lips,
charms a plenty
the way he kneads dough
always leaving flour on my cheek.
I have learned, love is found
in the leftovers, a baker's
dozen is never an accident.
Your daughters will never know
how to dance
without an orchestra,
engraved invitation,
or in bare feet
across the kitchen floor
where toe collides with toe,
and temperatures rise as flesh meets.

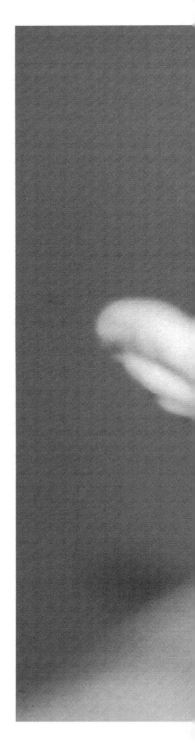

Karie McNeley

Thoughts on a Kissing Picture

I'm the one in the picture
that looks like a slightly romantic
version of anti-romantic everything,
pausing awkwardly to take a snapshot
of our smooching.

I raised my cell phone above our tangled heads
with my finger on the shutter button
and quickly snapped the photo,
smacking the moment with a mack truck flash.
Because if I didn't, the memory of your mouth
would slip off of my tongue much too easily.

So I freeze-framed the moment as my lips smooshed
like putty between the oceanic part of yours,
and my caterpillar eyebrows were caught mid-action
reaching from my forehead to tickle your face.

You were captured clumsy beautiful,
with smirking half-moon dimples,
your hair: a shuffled deck of cards,
and one eye partially opened,
accepting the temporary blindness
like a flattered deer in headlights.

Girl & Boy Feet

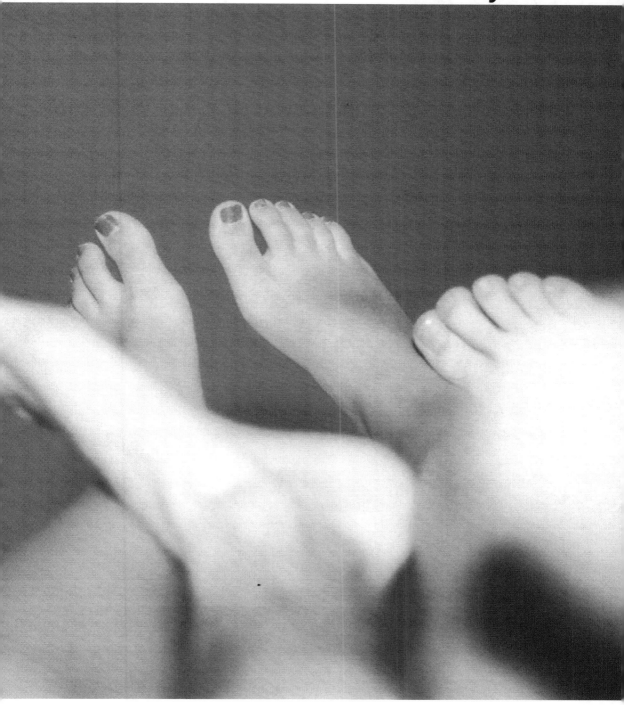

Deirdre Favreau
Enigma

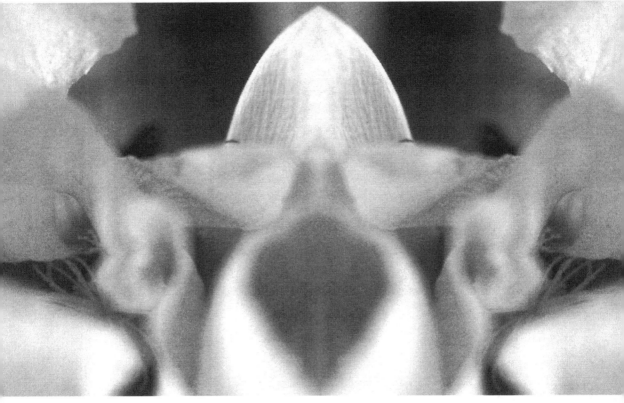

Karie McNeley
Flowers

Yeah, nobody cares.
Write a poem about sex.

Susana H. Case

Juana La Larga in Guatemala City, 1803

Tonight I light a candle in your memory,
Long Juana, examined by a court physician
for your *monstrous clitoris,* inch and a half.
No candle for Esparragosa, doctor-
philosopher who compared you to

the women of Egypt, by which he meant
exotic in *deformity* and *defect,*
who tried to arouse your monster to assess
its threat, grotesque handlings that
failed to inflame you. A clump of reeds,

female anatomy was. Is.
Newspapers published maps of approved-sized
parts. What did you think of the trial,
your acquittal? I hear only silence.
Tonight I light a candle to my freedom

under the sheets, to the freedom of all
women viewed as licentious—and to those
still not. In your time, many thought
only one sex existed—each of us with
male genitalia, hidden inside.

Overheated by men's work,
we would feel a penis pop out. Tonight
I light a candle to all surprises of the body.
Even then, some pronounce this foolish,
female determined by flame in the *heart.*

Jaclyn Weber

Modern Crop Circle

Somehow I've ended up here,
lying in a cornfield at 3AM
naked on a Western style blanket.
(I'm a Cali girl)
I figure this is what Midwesterners do...
have a romp in cornfields.
Yet he's a virgin.
(Saving himself) ←I figure that's what hip Christians call it.
If he can even still call himself that, since he's getting—

I'm getting ahead of myself,
telling this story without trying to describe
the way my freckles lined up with the constellations
or how his thumbs pressed into my back dimples.
^*Lying in a cornfield sounds rather romantic when I write it out like that*^
Really it's just trespassing, giving head and getting nothing in return
only understanding I'm not the one.
(Just for fun)

Somehow I'm ok with this
as he grasps my head towards his and pushes down
all the memories I've avoided.
Much rather lie here surround by Bloomington bushes
and mine exposed to the understanding
that so many other men have marked me with
(I'm good at pleasure)←A nicer term than slut

Not the marrying, cooking, pearl-wearing type of woman
he would take home to lie down on mattress sheets,
filled with feathers and promising forever.
I'm never getting any good guarantees,
just enough for this one time—

(And that second time) ←I was feeling lonely that week
when he Facebooked me and asked me
to lie in a cornfield, pretend it's romantic
and imagine the Cosmos beneath my freckles.

Elena Rodriguez
Belladonna of the Night

Kristina Shue

War Paint

I want to wear lipstick
and high heels and all that "girl" shit—
without being somebody's bitch,
without worrying about my tits
and how many stares they'll get, how many boxes
I'll be put into by the time I reach the end of the block.
I'm not a hooker, not a "slut," not interested
in your cock, please don't bring it up. I'm not
a gay man in drag, but damn, I want to be. Is that harsh of me?
I have enough white guilt to build nests
for all the sparrows in the city—with long strands of hair
I refuse to cut short to look "more..." I don't care
how you think I should look, or be. Don't you call me
on my "straight privilege," on my "passing privilege."
I don't want to pass as anything, but to light up my being
in every way short of screaming with affirmation
and enthusiasm: I *am*, and I am not static. This iron string
needs daily tuning—I have a good ear, and I do my best.

Taylor Wilson
Right Mind, Wrong Body

Erin Parker

Lost Life Found

She used to say she had to come out twice: the first time as a Lesbian and the second time as Butch. Now there's a third time. She had to come out as a Transgender man.

This isn't how our story was supposed to go.

For him, I suppose, it was like a rebirth. For me it was like helplessly watching her commit suicide in slow motion. She was up on a ledge threatening to jump. I listened at first. I talked to her. I tried to understand. I blamed myself for breaking up with her. If we'd stayed together, would she have gone ahead with this? I was desperate to save her. I cried when I was alone in my car or was sick in the bathroom at work. I was mourning her body that would be irrevocably altered and changed. And then I broke every rule I had and wrote the meanest, most scathing letter I could. I used everything I knew about her against her, rolled it all up in that letter and beat her hard with my words. My intention was to shock her, to wake her up, to devastate her into thinking clearly. I was convinced she hadn't thought this all the way through, that she was romanticizing what it meant to be a man.

I'd come out as a Lesbian because we were together and we were happy and I figured it was about time. Up until then, I had been okay with being a straight girl who had experimented a little. With her it was different. With her it was real. With her for the first time I could see for decades. We moved in together, we had a cat, we built a life. We had friends and holiday traditions. We held hands in public (unless we were in Orange County) and we had potluck dinners at our house. We saved up for her car and I polished her boots and then gave myself manicures. She bought me expensive lipstick. We went to museums together. We had a subscription to *Wine Spectator* magazine. We liked gourmet cheese and European chocolate. We had a massive collection of books that we constantly added to when there was a little extra money. We intentionally mixed our books together on our bookshelves. That's when we both knew it was serious, that we both trusted in our future together.

My identity was finally steadied by her. Because of all that made her Butch, I embraced being Femme, and that was much more of a homecoming. That's where I found the real power to become fearless. For the first time I saw my femininity as a strength instead of a weakness. I was in the spotlight, not the bullseye. I started wearing red lipstick and skirts of all lengths. She was right there beside me with jeans and t-shirts with rolled up sleeves, slicked back hair, work boots, her wallet on a chain. Dapper as always.

If she'd felt like a man all along, had I been in a straight relationship for a decade? Was I really just a straight girl in lipstick and heels who was with a man in disguise, a wolf in sheep's clothing, the ultimate Trickster? Where was the language for the edge I'd developed? Had any of it been real? I'd been had.

I knew sending that email meant the end of any friendship we had left, and I was willing to risk it to save her. If she would remain the person I knew, the Butch I had loved, she could hate me. As long as she still existed, was out there in the world, then that was okay with me. It was a small price to pay to shake her awake and save her from herself. Who says Femmes are selfish? Making her hate me was the most loving thing I ever tried to do.

I want to write about the painful beauty of the journey. Of finding one's place in the world, of real soul love that cooled to a supportive and respectful friendship. We were friends who were exes, who were tough as nails, who made a concerted and careful effort to be respectful of the past we shared, the life we'd once built. I want to write that we told each other how happy we were for the other now that we were with other people, living different lives, seeing each other blossom from a respectful distance, into who we were meant to become without each other and after our time together was over. I want to write about this, but it isn't what happened.

Sending the email of the most scathing letter I've ever written is the most shameful thing I have done. I knew it wouldn't change her mind. I knew it wasn't any of my business. And even though I knew it, I convinced myself I had to try. I saw myself clutching her hand, steadying her as she teetered on a ledge high above the ground. One slip, and she would fall. I would reach out to her, she would take my hand and I would help her down. I knew her. I knew everything about her. I knew her and so I could hurt her. I knew her and so I could save her. If my words were a hurtful betrayal, if they shocked her into inaction it would be worth it. She would still exist as herself. That's what I thought. I hit send, finally severing our tie.

She was up there on that ledge, and I could swear she was about to fall. What I couldn't understand until later, until I was alone in the aftermath and palpable silence after her raw, visceral reaction to my letter, was that she wasn't losing her balance and starting to fall. I could finally step back far enough to see. She was spreading her wings and starting to breathe. She was stepping off the ledge. Not to fall. But so he could fly.

Fernando Gallegos
The Three Graces

Clifton Snider

La Reina de Taos Pride & Pueblo

for Arius Damien Reyna

With stenciled eyebrows,
shaded green eye shadow
& full ruby-red lips,
she makes her entrance,
risen to her full height,
taller than any man
here in the Alley Cantina,
her own long black hair the length of her back,
in full-length black gown
with tapered & full-bodied green bodice,
a black velvet scarf &
sparkling rhinestone tiara,
earrings & necklace.

For photo ops
she removes her glasses
holds her head high
& to the right.

She knows who she is,
a queen observing her subjects,
her left hand & arm in a pink cast
from an accident.

                              She holds it erect;
her matching black purse dangles
by its handle from her wrist.

A white sash proclaims in bold black:
"MISS GAY PRIDE TAOS 2010."

She has risen from repressed tradition,
fabric of her own native culture,
two-spirit proclamation,
soul & sinew of her people.

—4 September 2010
Taos, New Mexico

Robin Steere Axworthy

History of Her

We start young.
A taunt –

Chicken.

In a corner of
a playground, a sunny field,
a room upstairs:
"Show me yours."

Head down,
she longs to run,
but lifts her skirt,
pulls the plain white panties down,
wanting something too,
unknown.

Emptied of words –
she will show them
her flat pale belly,
bare, shy pubis;
spindled legs
as shy as fawns.

Released from their regard,
she is not rewarded
with honor or wonder;
laughter drums her home;
she tells no one –

Chicken.

The next time will be a man
in a car who asks directions,
his swollen stake
surprising her into
stunned paralysis
until she breaks and runs –

Chicken.

Later it will be a boyfriend
opening his zipper
and guiding her hand there;
later still, it will be her head
forced down between his legs;
she will not say no –

Chicken.

If she's lucky,
she'll escape the teacher,
or her father's friend,
or the battering
in a dark room
where shouts and music
cover her cries;
she will tell no one –

Chicken.

She will find, eventually,
a man who says
he loves her and does,
but she can never
quite believe him,
fearing always
the snicker,
the pointing finger,
the shame
she cannot say –

Chicken.

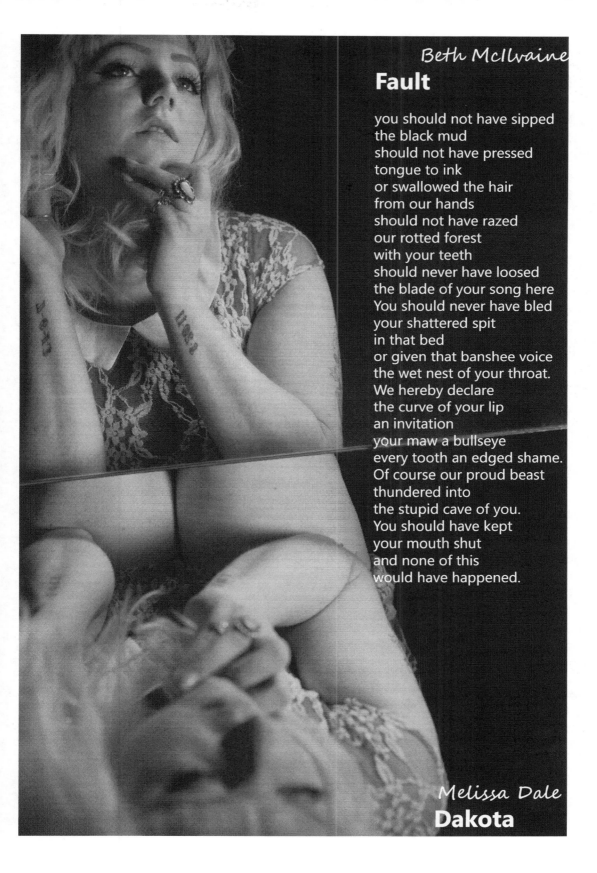

Beth McIlvaine

Fault

you should not have sipped
the black mud
should not have pressed
tongue to ink
or swallowed the hair
from our hands
should not have razed
our rotted forest
with your teeth
should never have loosed
the blade of your song here
You should never have bled
your shattered spit
in that bed
or given that banshee voice
the wet nest of your throat.
We hereby declare
the curve of your lip
an invitation
your maw a bullseye
every tooth an edged shame.
Of course our proud beast
thundered into
the stupid cave of you.
You should have kept
your mouth shut
and none of this
would have happened.

Melissa Dale

Dakota

Karla Cordero

A Spanish to English Translation on Sweet Things Gone Sour

Chicle: gum. tree skin. bubble breath. elastic sap. bad breath killer. teeth. chew. gum before first kiss. swallow gum. first kiss. he aggressive. say no. continue to say no. if he doesn't listen rip his right ear. turn knuckles into machetes. fight with your teeth. scream fire not rape. rip his left ear. whisper his mothers name slow. turn legs into pitchforks. if all else fails rub bobby pins like twigs. make fire. smoke signals. light his body on fire. cremation is survival.

Terry Ann Wright

Wonder Woman

Of course they still ask me
to pick out presents for
their girlfriends.

Superman needs some advice:
what should he say
when Lois cries for no reason?

Iron Man wants to know
what will get spots
out of his armor.

Aquaman asks me
if I would be interested
in going for a swim.

The Legion of Doom
won't shoot at me because
it's no fair, hitting a lady.

The Avengers won't
ask for my help, because
who wants help from a girl?

They all love the invisible plane,
of course. They want to see me
get ready for bed.

Who needs a golden lasso
to bind someone to the truth?
I hear it all day long.

So long, suckers. I'm taking
my invisible jet and checking out.
Good luck with your girlfriends.

You'll need it.

Terry Ann Wright

An Education

He picked me for my softness.

He wanted so badly to put his hands on it and crush it,
to chew on it, spit it out, grind it under his feet.

You could see it in the way he was rough with me:
the sensual, trembling desire just barely held back—

he wanted so badly to burn me, to light me on fire,
to crumple me in his fists;
one tire iron and I would be dead.

Hurting me was his drug;
he needed like the worst drink ever
to relocate that pain onto another body.

An engineering project: like an electrical current,
she might have been the start of it,
but he needed to close the circuit by making me the end of it.

Or mere physics, really:
he needed to take the violence of her swing
and let it move through him onto me.

Or maybe it was religion: so he could walk away,
I bore the burden of her sins.
I was his Christ on the cross.

No wonder he kept telling me "that doesn't hurt"—because
by the transfer of his pain to me,
it didn't.

Rose Mary Neff
Counterpart

Open Letter

Dear guys who crossed the street when you saw me walking my dog at 11 PM,

Thank you. No, honestly: thank you.

I don't know why you decided to cross the empty street when you saw me standing there waiting for my little dog to do his business. Maybe you didn't want to deal with sharing the sidewalk. Maybe you didn't want to have to say hello or acknowledge me in any way.

I don't know why you crossed the street, but thank you. It made me feel safer when you did.

You see, I have to be aware of every man who walks past me in public, especially at night, because unfortunately I cannot tell if you're a good person just by looking at you. I have to be careful.

You both saw me almost a block away and decided—for whatever reason—to give me space. You nonchalantly crossed the street and continued on your way as if nothing had ever happened. As someone who has to worry about her interactions with men so that she doesn't "give the wrong idea" or "send mixed signals" and as someone who often has to deal with and "accept" harassment based on my perceived gender, I appreciate men who go out of their way to make me feel safe, especially in public spaces.

You probably thought nothing of your actions. You never even got close enough to see me very well, though my shape and figure make it obvious to most people that I'm a woman, no matter what I'm wearing. Well, I want to let you know that it really meant something to me. It was a relief. It meant that I could breathe easier, even if it was for just a moment.

Thank you,
Viannah

Karla Cordero

Instructions on How to Avoid a Disaster

Be a girl with careful heart. Too many hungry men. Grandmother says they eat their women raw. Pulpit molars. Spit chipped red nail polish like sun flower seed. So kiss hard. Keep your index on trigger. If he looks like salvation, if he speaks in symphony, ask for his mother's middle name. Refuse the jewelry. All pearls from his palms will hide bear trap & play you deer. Turn to the nearest exit. Run. Jump fence. Recite bible verse backwards. Men will hunt you still by bloodhound. Avoid floral perfume. Smear mud on your lips. Let worms do all the work. & remember keep running. Wait for the man who speaks your name slow, touching only parts of you made for picking flowers.

Rose Mary Neff
Lola

Kristina Shue

Undress Me

after Sandra Cisneros

The straight, white Midwestern woman in me, the planning-for-the-future
in me—you unlock them from the back of my buried subconscious. The
naming-my-children in me. The decorating-our-home and the autumn
baking in me. The apron-wearing and back-to-school lunch-packing in me.
The nostalgia of my mother in me. The bouquets of fresh-cut tulips from
composted, nail-dug flower beds in me. You fold up the leaves
of dictionaries dog-eared on terms I think define me. Close the cover
on *bisexual, straight-edge, female-assigned at birth*. On lists of *-phile*
and *-ist* and figures of my discipleship. On all the *semi-* of my shifting
self-inventory. You rush me back to simpler lines, or where lines
do not exist. To my tomboy, my punk, my career-woman costumes
and undress me, wipe off candy-colored war paint with your thumb,
slide thorns from my cheekbones. You bring out the natural highlights
in me. You shake me like a snow globe with each touch of your all-senses
glance and make me dance like each flake, the wave and discrete
of a sugared blizzard.

G. Murray Thomas

Give Me Real Boobs

Hey! I'm sick of all these plastic boobs.
You know, the kind that leap out of the top of the dress
and shout, "Hi honey. I'm home!"
Give me real boobs.

I don't require massive proportions:
A sudden Paricutin erupting out of your farmlands.
A single sentence overwhelming
everything else your body has to say.

And I don't demand perfection:
Two exactly spherical globes,
each with a single Mount Everest.

No, I like boobs with some reality,
individuality,
personality,
humanity.

The same things I like
in the rest of a woman.

Frank Kearns

Girl Power

After decades of we same men
growing old together in the same stale offices
girls have arrived at the aerospace firm

they are just graduated and mostly grown up
smart   a boost to diversity metrics
and with them comes all sorts of awkwardness

they are bleary-eyed casual sometimes on Monday
other times gussied up way too much
for we dinosaurs nursing our aging hearts

they drape decorations on cubicle walls
wear costumes to meetings at Halloween
call for tequila shots at the Christmas luncheon

they have started to learn what has to be done
and now are beginning   from time to time
to express their opinion on how we should do it

and after weeks of sweat on a major proposal
the young women working on chapters and figures
that the old guys send back all marked up in red

the word goes out that we won the contract
and before the leaders can gather the team
shouts of *girl power* echo from the cubicles

Elena Rodriguez

Belladonna of the Night

Jan Presley

Clitoridectomy

The elimination of clitoridal sexuality is a necessary
precondition for the development of femininity.
—Sigmund Freud, 1925

Where the body branches into thighs
a seed rests, deceptively small,
sends tendrils deep up in the trunk
to web the stomach, the heart, the skin,
the mouth.   We want
to link a sweetness to this seed;
seed of a sugar date or dark cherry.
When it blossoms we are drunk
with thick honey. Wet and flaming,
it swells to a taproot the body cannot hold.
Enters the brain, renders us
well-fed, useless, happy.
If we pull the seed out where it rests
like a bad tooth from the jaw,
bad berry from the bowl,
if we remove it like a damaged limb,
do the roots curl in the body like a useless hand,
thick and dull as a mute tongue?
Are we haunted by a phantom blossom of hunger?
A phantom feast?

Michael Cantin

"Not All Men," or, "I'm sorry, I will let you finish, but first we need to address that this poem is really about MY balls."

Now look, I understand that you have a valid argument. I get it, really I do, but the fact of the matter is that you've somehow offended me. And I matter. And I matter because I am a man child.

I get that you are saying that it is not right that women are being threatened with horrible actions and being harassed, and that this is being done by men. I get it, really I do, but the fact of the matter is that you've somehow offended me. And I matter. And I matter because I have these balls.

These balls hanging low are easily offended from the scaffolding of my privilege. Not that I have privilege. Sure, some men have privilege. All of those white men. Those white white men who don't understand.

But I do understand, and I am going to let you finish, I totally will. I get that you are saying that it is not right that women are being threatened with horrible actions and being harassed, and that this is being done by men. I get it, really I do, but the fact of the matter is that you've somehow offended me.

And I matter. And I matter because I have these balls.

And you really should pay attention to these balls.
These educated massive balls.
These Not All Men Balls.

These balls hanging low are easily offended from the scaffolding of my privilege. Not that I have privilege. I'm sorry, I will let you finish, but first we need to address that this poem is really about MY balls. I was raised by a woman. A woman who is a mother, and I am sure you have met her at some point. So, because I was raised by a wonderful intelligent woman, I don't have privilege.

I mean, just look at these balls!

These educated massive balls. These balls are feminist balls,
and by that I mean they are academic feminist balls, not some
simpering Tumblr feminist balls. I am so above these other men.

I mean, just look at these balls! These educated massive balls.
These balls hanging low are easily offended from the scaffolding
of my privilege. Not that I have privilege. And again, I'm sorry, I will
let you finish, but first we need to address that this poem is really
about MY balls.

These Not All Men balls.
These balls being far far more important than you realize.
And so you really should be paying attention to them.
I mean, right fucking now.
Look at me!
Listen!
This is all about me
and my balls!

Why are you getting mad?

Terry Ann Wright

Something Good

I liked to watch you eat, he says. *You ate with such gusto. Oh man! And you know what* that *means.* The leer is in his voice, but I know he also means it affectionately. Kindly. He means most things kindly. He asked me once about the time in my life when I did not eat passionately, in fact, I passionately did not eat. We're only starting to get to know each other and so he doesn't yet know that if he wants a real answer, he has to ask twice.

The real answer is it was *fantastic.* No one wants to hear that answer. Sure, I looked terrible, so terrible friends asked my roommate if I had cancer. The funniest thing about that is I have no idea what I looked like. I only know what I felt. When I lay in bed I could cup my hand over my hipbone. Even today my hand flutters there, seeking some solid evidence of what others would call hollowness. But I can tell you what I see in the mirror today seems the same to me.

I can still recite the litany of what I would eat, I suppose like others can recite the prayers for each bead of their rosary. Oh Holy Monday: I would eat half a muffin. Tuesday, nothing. Wednesday, half a yogurt. Thursday, nothing. Friday, an apple. Well, half an apple. And so on. You'd be surprised how long you can do that before others catch on, and maybe you'd be surprised how powerful you feel. How powerful I felt: everyone wanted me to do something, and I said, no. I did it all my way. Still, after a while it draws attention and you might be surprised that attention isn't what I wanted. So the answer was simple: like a soldier on the beachhead, under fire, obeying the orders in his bones before he senses them in his mind: switch tactics.

Of course I am the only person I know who can't make herself throw up by forcing a finger down her throat. Oh! I tried! Oh I tried and tried and the effort: I cried and cried. Another failure. Slick hands covered with saliva and tears. But people are resourceful, and all you have to do is trot off to the drugstore and buy a few things like you're stocking a first aid kit, and buy things that come to your aid. And just like my palm still draws over my hipbone, my fingers can still curl around the sense memory of a tiny brown bottle.

I've always been good at following directions, so I did indeed chase the tablespoon with a glass of warm water. A full glass of warm water. Just the other day I refused a warm bottle of water, because just the thought makes ancient muscle memory stir. I say stir: it's not a stirring. In fact it is violent. I realize now that violence is something I conflated with passion; a yearning to be consumed, not consume. Research shows it *causes the convulsion of the alimentary canal.* Convulsion: yes. The sibilance does recall the rush of fluids such violence produces. The first time, I combined my ability to follow directions with my impatience with delayed reaction, and doubled the dose.

Some might call that a mistake. And when the first wave hit, just as I was leaving the house, I thought, oh, hmmm. Maybe this was a mistake. An hour later, I was sure it was not. It was not a mistake. It was salvation. It was everything I wanted to say, and more (and more): I was so sick of everything my life was, of everything I did and said, everything that wasn't said or done, that the only sane response was violent rejection. How I wish I could convey the utter consumption of every fiber of your body, convulsing, rejecting, rejecting, rejecting. So an hour later the seizures subsided and I rose in front of the bathroom mirror, bright red, covered in sweat, and more triumphant than I have ever felt then or since. I had the key. That viscous amber liquid would save me. And that's the secret: I would do it all again tomorrow.

So, yes, I eat with gusto. I still plan my life around the next time I can eat something good. Let's call it an early lesson in how one passion can be used to replace another. Though, I have yet to find a passion that can consume me so completely. Except, the other day I got a sunburn and today the skin between my shoulder blades is a ripe peach, and all I want in the world is to feel his hands hold my shoulders, his lips kiss my back.

Rose Mary Neff

I Am You

Charlotte San Juan

Zhōng Xìng

This word, she says,
we use to describe
those kinds of women—
those women
with the really short
hair, like a boy's.
Those women in pressed
suit jackets, dark pants,
granite faces, leather
briefcases. They
are their own husband.
Neutral gender,
she says. Neutral
faces. I've seen
these plain-faced women
at the metro stations,
their log-stalk legs
spread a wide berth,
the way they pock
the ground with spit,
and let loose a wide sneer,
give wary men cold
eyes, I have never
found anything more
frightening, more
beautiful.

Mother

Jackie Joice
Dollhouse

Christine Brandel

A Wife Is A Hope Chest

A wife is a hope chest in which you keep
the things you will need for a good life.
1: A kettle. Tie the cord to her wrist, she should
never be out of its reach. 2: A snapshot of the woman
you wish you had married. Push it through her
eyes, put it in her head. 3: A pen knife. Good
for cutting bread, package strings, the ring
from her finger. 4: Coins. They will make sounds
so you know when she's coming. 5: Silence.
Do not read the letters she writes you, do not
speak even if she pleads. 6: Cotton wool. To stop
the flow. Because she will bleed. 7: A book.
One heavy hardback you never intend to read.
8: A skeleton key. Trust her. She won't use it to get out.

Amy Wright

Dusting

Dusting the furniture in the house where I grew up
as a favor to my mother during my now-thrice
yearly visit, I follow the mantle clock's
curve, slide my palm over the lip
of the washstand, trace the icebox's oak panels,
scent of lemon oil, feel of damp
cotton, one of my old cloth diapers, in hand & tenderness
for things kept longer than me, in some cases
longer than forty-two years of marriage.
The piano stool where I pored over sheets
of Beethoven, Franz Gruber,
so she could have carols decking our holiday halls,
small offering of a Niagara Falls thimble,
a rosewood Jerusalem Communion goblet
where she tucked a centimeter-long splinter
that went into my father. She saves things
to show me, the fired birdhouse
she bought for its odd pattern,
the fan pull made of teak and mahogany.
I even sweep the waxy cloth over the spice
rack's top ledge the way she taught me,
the full length of each walnut rocker runner
like the back of my teeth.

Alison Stone

Haunting

A giant spider crouches by the door.
Moans grow louder
in the darkness, one green
glowing finger reaches out. The other mom
and I shriek, recoil from a doll
mummified in toilet paper, red
paint in teacups, plates of river rocks
meant to be bones.
Were you scared? For real? my daughter asks,
giggling with her friend, both girls
paint-smeared and shining, unaware
this morning a politician said
women who earn as much as men
have trouble finding husbands.
I want to chain them here, safe
among monsters of their own making,
before lipstick and self-loathing and silence.
Above them, a vampire her older brother
built spreads his wings.

Lori McGinn

Mist settles in her bones
She is dreaming in the damp night

Each day awakens and hangs there
Heavy as a radiation apron

The phone is an empty source
No comfort or color on the electric line

Only this dark drawn stout
Thick on my tongue like molasses

Comfort comes in the yellow gold of sunset
Purple flowers line the fence

The buzz of the bees unsettle me
The roar falls on deaf ears

The undercurrent of a big wave is rippling the earth
Throats open in silent screams

There is a little girl picking pink carnations
There is false safety in the flow of the hills

She cannot see the wolf, the red in his eyes
The forest falling asleep

Daniel McGinn

Flower Child

I was a handle in search of a plow
I was a hunger in need of a horse
I was a huntsman, a bringer of seeds
She was the bluebird on God's green shoulder
She was born a broken promise
She brought stories to the fire

Once upon a time she spent her time
liberating flowers from rich folk's gardens
Flowers were the money she was planning to spend
She broke loose in a puff of smoke
She went flying on a flick of ash
She went winding down a mountain road
She rode the skids on a hair pin curve

She was a fast driver
a good girl with really great hair
a glimpse of heaven in a see-through top
When we met we just were
and it just was and it was good
and all of a sudden we were always there

Once her porch-light eyes came on for me
Once she started calling me home
Once I fell in love with her beautiful face
Once upon a time we both looked good
Once it happened we didn't even blink
We could make a black couch blush
We hit it so hard we popped out the shower doors
We did it in the garden and we did it on the mountain
We did it by the lake and we did it in the water
We made the blue sky blue
We did it and we did it and we had twin sons

Pink blossoms bloomed in the almond tree
We did it again and had a baby girl
Flower petals fell and landed in our yard
Flower petals landed on the foot path to her door
Flower petals fell and planted perfume at her feet

Daniel McGinn
Pretty Lori at the Lake

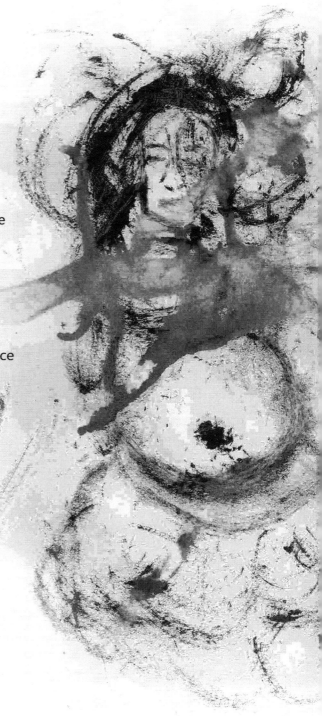

Christina Foskey
The one with untamed hair

I watch a woman in a kitchen
blind hands find
tomatoes, chilies, cilantro
she's unloading market buys alone
the turkey already in the oven
the one that works, in the garage

I watch a woman work in grays
she bats at kitchen flies
finding their way in through a window
her husband hasn't fixed in years
mumbling under her breath
she receives a kiss atop her short frame
from a returning son
"*Pan Con Pollo?*" he asks
she looks up at him and only smiles

I learn from a woman
that she says, "I love you"
by fixing a meal with the same care
in which her hands touch her lover's face
right before he says,
"honey, I'm going out with the boys."

her mastered house help hands
form bunches of watercress and chop
sliced angles of cucumbers and stop
she garnishes plates
with the colors of her home
la hermosa salvadorena

I watch a woman plain-faced
folding turkey meat
into pale *bolillo* rolls with dark hands
in the same somber way
she once tucked her five sons into bed
pouring over them
warm, red hope
asking herself...
"Is this enough?"

Danielle Mitchell

Interview with Sister [Age 44]

Who am I without you & the open-heart system of your dining room table?
The daughters gathered there, little birds in their breasts all fluttering &
wide mouthed. Teach me your lessons from the vacuum. In the absence
of our mother you are my mother. In your memory I'm always a woman. A
little reflection of yourself come early. Before the girls began to grow inside
you & we planted the willow in the backyard beside your pond to remind
you of our grandmother—& now those girls, long & weepy, sprout in their
new bodies by the pool. Where did your longing go? When did you know
that your young sister was full of wings & light & forgetting the absence
she needed you for. Laid in the yard, wanting to be in your image to nest
& go & the kitchen & the side yard where the muse keeps caged always at
least one beautiful bird of prey. Why are you always so busy? How do you
keep the days as they tumble out from clogging at your feet? Like prayers.
Like groceries. What are we if not the answer to the other.

Dr. Ernest Williamson III

African American Pregnant Actuality

Sheila Cooper

Choices

Ring on her finger, toddler on her hip,
she stands in line at the local market,
arms laden with cukes and tomatoes,
pondering tonight's dinner.
It has to be something quick;
she's volunteering all evening
for the campaign.
She's got fifty essays to grade,
and brownies to bake for the PTA.
She pulls on her Seven jeans, hoodie,
black boots,
hooks in her silver hoops, and
sweeps her hair up in a curly ponytail.
She kisses her man
and the babies goodnight and
heads out the door,
                    black feminist.

Annie Freewriter

I'm Boyish

Moses is what I named my doll—not Barbie.
I would glance at my reflection
in other girls' patent leather shiny shoes.

My baby sister wailed—head hanging
a bully was taking her trike.
Pushing his face on the ground, I said, "Say uncle."

At twelve and thirteen, I rode my bike,
my trusty steed—to conquer the jungles
of Glassell park with my lion-dog Terry.

I set up armies of Chinese marbles and shot them
with my thumb and pointer finger.
Both sides won.

I dug tunnels, bridges and roads
for my trucks and cars
in the planter box dirt.

At fifty-five I cut down a tree
with my handsaw—I felled goliath
red-faced and sweaty—triumphant.

Raquel Reyes-Lopez

Scraped

Was it because I knocked a baby hummingbird
from its nest when I was seven? Was that wrong?

Did the angels snitch on me
when they saw how I forced
that tiny little thing to fly?

Did they tell God or was he already watching?
Did God forget I jumped a five-foot wall to save
the hummingbird from those boys?

Does he remember my scraped knees?
Does he think about the blood like I do?

Did he smile when I offered the baby hummingbird
to my mother as a gift? Or did he smile when mother
refused to cage the hummingbird and plopped it back
into its nest?

Why is it six months after my miscarriage I keep
dreaming hummingbird memory over and over?
Is this God's way of talking to me?

Does he think about the blood like I do?
Tell me, does he think about the blood
like I do?

Will December 1st be beautiful?
Will it snow somewhere?

When will hummingbirds teach me
how to fly backwards?

Kelsey Bryan-Zwick
Portrait of Frida

Elmast Kozloyan

Vole: To Fly

I
Being graceful is strenuous work
Arms in second
feet in first
So deep in turn out
I'm turned around
Lift
Ouch   is a complete sentence
He pas de chevaled in my stomach
and jetéd into this world

II
He had my legs
Blond like his father
I rinsed his hair in flat champagne
so it would stay golden
even after he would be told
boys don't wear pointe shoes

III
I bought them anyway
Toes cracked
carrying our full body weight
on wooden blocks
He had less to bear
for the time being

IV
When you pirouette
push down
feet parallel fourth
arms straight sixth
Pick a spot
on the wall
in the mirror
at the thing you love most
Keep your eyes on it at all times
If you look away
you will fall

Sarah ChristianScher

In Defense of Barbie

I.
My Nonnie gave me Barbies
every gift-giving holiday the doll and I would stare at each other
separated by miles of thin plastic
our smiles fixed and painful
I said thank you and moved on to the next present

Once Barbie and I were alone I stripped her
of clothes and stereotypes
she became spy and soldier
she rode naked
barebacked astride stuffed animals
to lay siege to She-Ra's castle

II.
I wondered why Nonnie gave her to me
relegated after age 10 to lives of collecting dust
stacked unceremoniously on the highest shelf of my closet
or buried deep in our garage

to me, Barbie was a mark of shame
a toy I hid from my male playmates for fear of being labeled "a boring girl"
unfit for rough fun and baseball in the street
it wasn't until Nonnie died that I wondered
what was Barbie to her?

III.

Nonnie was in the first generation of girls to hold Barbie
to see a doll not as a baby
but as a woman upright and independent

Nonnie was a single mother
raising two boys and a girl
with little money left after food and housing

Nonnie's name is Barbara

I won't condone Barbie's poor choices
made again and again
as if they too were factory-produced
I won't excuse her unrealistic proportions
but I will say something in defense of Barbie
Barbie is her own woman
is not beholden to Ken for anything
raises her sister alone
has time for her friends
maybe there's still hope for Barbie after all

Mary Torregrossa

Samurai Mother

*after the legend of the goddess Benzaiten
who tamed the dragon of Enoshima Island*

Black sand iron ore makes the blade,
forged with charcoal in the kiln.
Hammer the red hot block
in the fire of the furnace
until it shines new born.

I chisel my name
into the cold flat edge
smooth as satin trim,
sharp as first love lost.

When I call to it, it comes to me.

In her amniotic ocean
daughter waits at the portal,
her fingertips strum the lining
of my womb. Warrior Mother
ripples like water in the wind,
traces petals at the hilt of the sword,
slices the air with the long katana.

And when the dragon comes
to devour the village children
on the Island of Enoshima,
scales flexing blue-green,
teeth like broken quartz
charring tongue and cat's eye

I will slay it twice, until the steel
samurai rings like a guillotine.

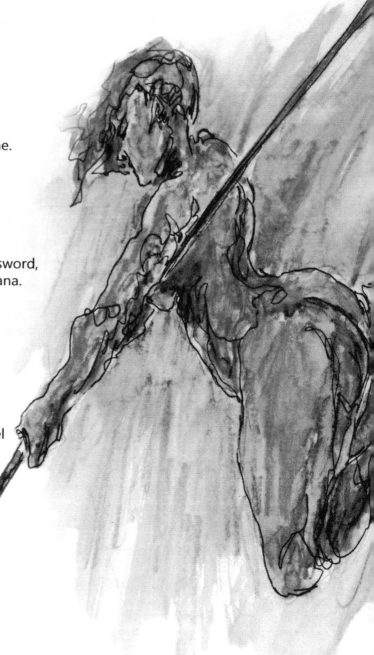

Nancy Lynée Woo

Memory Machine

Science says that the memory of our ancestors
may be passed down through genes.

That mice electrocuted to fear the scent of cherry blossoms
have offspring who also fear cherry blossoms.

My grandfather had a red beard.
Never knew his mother.

His mother.
Spat him out and gave him away.
Or they took him away.

Lost in the backwards of time,
the rape never recorded.

Around 1915 in some small village
eastward from here.

The men, taught to conquer.
Conquistadors we called them.
Their glory, our wombs.

Why I cringe
when a man much larger than me
scowls, perhaps my DNA remembers
the scent of cherry blossoms wilting.

Fernando Gallegos

She fought for love

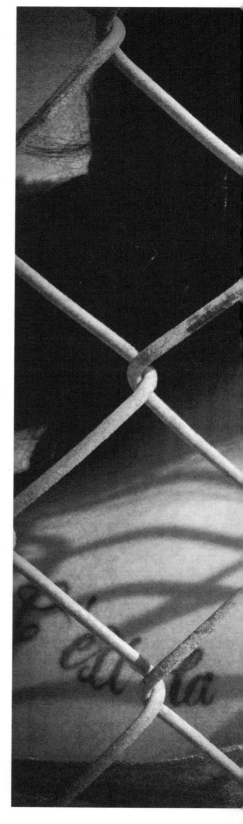

Sharon Elliott

Ratatattoos

for my daughter Hannah
  (who had many tattoos and committed suicide)

across her arms a murder of crows
in raucous obsidian flight

around her back barren fields
with stubble of harvested wheat
a gruff beard on a translucent chin
her lover
caught like an urban bandit
stealing cars
stealing whiskey
stealing her heart

pooled under her left shoulder blade
a crystal blue lake
touching a night horizon
destination to the flocking crows

in the dent of her buttocks
peeking out like a sparkle of precious stone
a single orange poppy
the stem disappearing between the cheeks
the flower nodding its delicate head as she walks

each needle painting on her skin
signifying the pleasure and pain
of being alive

Claire Ibarra
The Other Side

Peggy Dobreer

The Things My Father Gave Me

No Bat Mitzvah, on my thirteenth birthday,
an unnecessary expense in America. You
have to join a temple, that's a pretty penny
for a girl. Instead a small white box, a delicate
chain, enameled Star of David, circled in gold.
"Girls like jewelry," my father said.

On my sweet sixteen, expecting jewelry, I
received The Odes of Horace, modern translations,
Latin text included, plus the announcement
of expectations, four full years of study.
It'll make you a fine speller...and just what's
needed, should you want to be a doctor. Also
a set of rules for dating was put forth. The boy
with the bicycle, and the English Setter, later
to become one of the richest in Forbes, was not
up to father's standards. He wasn't up to mine
either, but that is beside the point.

Tobi Alfier

The Divorce

Dear ~~soon-to-be-ex~~ husband, I want ~~you out of the house~~ to write poems that make people feel that life is worth living and that means I need you to leave. I want ~~your body hair reeking of cigar smoke out of my bed~~ to stop sleeping with the undertone of the Golf Channel in my ears all night. Please stop criticizing ~~everything I do, from the way I drive to the way I breastfed~~ the movies I like, subtitles are lovelier than explosions. And my books? Let's not compare Stephen King to Yeats, okay? You are a ~~bully~~ difficult husband but an excellent father. Even your son says "Dad is ~~an ass~~ a really great guy, do you think you will ever get back together?" But I don't think that is possible ~~not in a million years, not if you came crawling back apologizing because I know you wouldn't mean it~~. I do wish you luck, yes ~~you have stolen a decade of my life~~ we were married for ten years and that counts for something ~~nothing, get your goddamn shirts out of my closet. I had to use the closet in the other room when you lived here, I want my closet back!~~ Best of luck to you ~~fuck you, and by the way, shave that stupid goatee off, you look like you have a pussy on your face~~ and I hope we can always be friends. I will live the life I want to write ~~without you, thank God~~ and let's be the best parents we can be for our son ~~as usual I will do everything I can to make up for your shortcomings and you will blame me for undermining your authority~~.

xo

Sabrina Fedel

Play Like a Girl

My daughter plays hockey. She loves it. She especially loves to play goalie, although she also likes to play forward. She's a pretty good little goalie, too. Good enough that, when a boys' peewee team from her organization needed a goalie, they recruited her, even though they had a boy goalie willing to play.

To be fair, it isn't just a boys' team. There are four other girls on it. There are really two types of teams through high school: coed and girls only. Girls-only hockey exists because, ultimately, the girls are forced out of the coed teams because of the brutality of the checking. Most girls are not physically willing or able to play coed hockey at the bantam level (13–14 years old) and above because that's when checking kicks in. So even though it may technically be a coed team, most parents of hockey-playing kids, including myself, refer to these coed teams as boys' teams.

I was worried about my girl playing on a boys' team this year. I was worried because I have seen boys' teams who did not treat their girl players very well. I have seen boys target girls on the opposing team. I have even known of parents encouraging their boys to "go after" girls on the opposing team. Moreover, because my daughter is a goalie, I worry about boys who might shoot high on her, trying to hit her in the head to intimidate her. Or just plain hurt her. Some people in hockey call that "buzzing the tower."

So every time my daughter goes out on the ice, I wonder what I should say to her (besides "protect your head at all costs"). The first game she played this year against another coed team, I made her tuck her pony tail into her jersey. "Don't make it obvious," I told her. Maybe I've been around the military too long, but I still remember the signs in a recruiting station in Dorchester, England, that my husband and I saw when we were there in 1995: "Travel inconspicuously" and "Don't let anyone know you are a Royal Marine." The Brits were well versed in avoiding terrorist attacks long before we caught on, thanks to the Irish Republican Army. Anonymity is sometimes your best defense.

My daughter is navigating a man's world. She is worth 77 cents to every dollar her brothers can make. She will go to college in the wake of shocking revelations about the pervasiveness of sexual assault on our university campuses, so much so that the federal government has stepped in. She will walk down the street and get cat-called, and no man who watches it will stand up for her. She will be harassed at every road construction site she drives through until she is at least thirty-five and sporting a car seat or two in her vehicle. She will have to thoroughly vet the boys who want to be her friends until she can trust them. She will know to never walk alone at night, no matter what. She will know to never accept a drink from someone she doesn't trust, literally, with her life. She will know that she needs to be able to support herself, and her children, in the event she chooses unwisely. She will know that she will always have to do more, work harder, and be braver than any man in her life.

But she will also know that she is an advocate. For herself and for every other woman who doesn't have a voice, or who allows her voice to be silenced or subjugated to the policies of people who try to make her a second-class citizen. She will know that she should be proud to be a woman, in every sense of the word, because women are mothers and leaders and teachers and givers. She will know that she descends from suffragists and scholars and artists and free thinkers. And she will know that she must conduct herself in a way that lifts up women everywhere and inspires the girls who come after her.

So when my daughter went out on the ice this weekend with her boys' team at a tournament in Cleveland, with her long, brown ponytail hanging down the outside of her jersey, I had only one piece of advice for her. I told her to play like a girl.

Karen S. Córdova

My Daughter with Waves Curling Red on White Beach of Her Shoulders

My daughter's jade eyes flicker ruby. When mad,
my daughter's nose flares like a stallion, like mine.
My daughter's tongue lassos her children, saddles them
ready to trot, dressage, high jump.
My daughter has flexible shoulders that swim through a torrent,
carrying babies, who think she's a mermaid enjoying the ride.
Who think mother's arms are their own private nest
with flesh curtains and velvet lap covers.
My daughter has waterfall hands from which salmon jump
into Béarnaise, and popovers fall onto prime rib shores.
Jeweled waterfall hands from which whirlpools of azurite,
topaz and knotted pearls foam into vortices—earrings
and necklaces fit for any Aphrodite neck.
My daughter's legs give Mercury a run for his dime
in hailstorm of work and creation.
My daughter has feet of steel mettle
that sing silver when she laughs.

Peggy Dobreer

Color Me Gray

The boundaries of my world mingle with hers,
one house, one home. Two hearts entrained
by proximity and absence of intrusion. She
was fashioned from my flesh. Now, we have
been delivered in a spin onto the platform of
her approaching self.

She is champing at the bit, ready to mount
the carousel of next exploration, jumping on
at any given moment. I am loath to stand
outside the lines. Color me gray when things
appear too black and white in her world. She
never seems to give much information.

The golden threads of her childhood to my
mystical marsupial pouch are frayed. She is
stepping away. Her culture holds the needs
of mine in contempt. I am ancient, dim-witted
in her mind. She is magnificent, fearless, and
fragile in mine. I would swaddle her for comfort
and protection but my arms no longer reach
around her widening expectations.

I am crackling, slow walking, back-looker. She
is fired up peeling into tomorrow, still
only present to just what is at hand, even
changing direction at the very moment of inception.
Nothing is consistent, love is constant.

I am obsolete. She is invention. I am polarized.
She is all systems go, leaping forward, throwing
down, full throttle, wide open. I am hands
folding in my lap. Much as I am able, I am letting go.

Tari Gunstone

Woman in the Raw

Trista Domingu
Plucking Eyebrows

You taught me how to
pluck my eyebrows, the
trick you said was to try
and not make one look
like the other. You would
know, the little old ladies
in your neighborhood
paid you penny per brow
as you went door to door.

Now lying in your hospital
bed you tell me they won't
let you shave your legs. I
never even knew they could
grow hair like mine, smooth
they were dangling from
your white La-Z-Boy turned
yellow from Kool cigarettes.

The scent of leather, minty
tobacco, and coffee bring
tears to my eyes now.

I made your legs smooth
again and rubbed them with
your favorite lotion. Then
fed you the stew I made just
for you, because though they
won't let you shave your legs
salt is now okay for you to
consume.

They gave you a year, but as
always you had other plans,
leaving this place days later
with smooth legs and salt upon
your tongue.

116

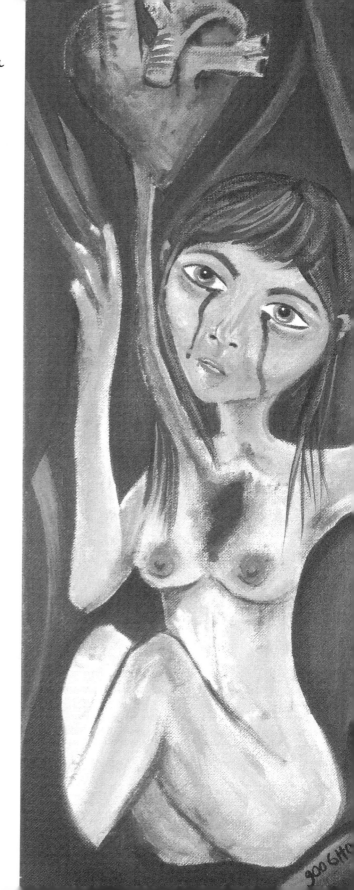

Christina Foskey

The tulips are too red
in the first place—
after Sylvia Plath

A promise makes no doctor
sails a sea of blue over my body
minimally invasive

Key hole in the seam
anchors down, down
conducts drooping tulips

Spilling sharp serenades
their unforgiving red
filament of me

Pelvis propped up bloated
an over flowing vase
my body sings of death

Inflated internal O's
O's of my mother, her mother, of me
adhesions burned and the
            womb

    just sits there

Angelita Ortega
Blues of Love

Dana Anastasia
Eggs

I dreamt of eggs last night:
a fertile prophecy.
Thick white shells cracking
over and over
spilling mucus suns
into my empty hands.

Toti O'Brien
What Is Love

Amanda Rochelle Martin

Eight Weeks

Silly of me to think it was my choice
when the pink line on the stick
registered in my mind.

I remember contemplating
whether I should continue
to harvest your existence

or have you sucked out
by the vacuum like the cells
and dirt holding to the carpet.

It was so silly of me to think
it was my choice. I chose
to let you grow little lemon

but I've learned I am not the one
with control. The universe
is indifferent was all I could say

when they pulled you, lifeless
lemon, from my tree and took
you far away where I can't follow.

JL Martindale

Afterbirth

Swaddled baby finally sleeps after hours of shrieking.
Hours of comforting: failed.
Holding, shushing, kissing, crying bled me dry.

My hair, crusty with drool,
with milk, with the grease of exhaustion
and this growing sense of dread.

Breasts ache despite being empty.
Scars are throb like ulcerating wounds.
And I'm tired. I'm so unbelievably tired.

Husband: home from work: he claws at me.
His touch demanding, unsympathetic, begging:
Hands on my ass. Hands on my tits.
His presumptuous kiss lingers too long;
starved, self-entitled lips press too hard
and that overeager tongue forces its way in.

I want to lock my body, hide it away and weep.
I want to find a dark hole in which to die.

I tell him this. And I cry.
I cry because I cannot stop the baby from crying.
I cry because I feel so lonely, deserted
in this hollow hell called motherhood.
I cry because he doesn't get what the "big deal" is.
I cry and I tell him this, but I don't think he hears me.
His desperate digits still dig at my flesh.

He says, "You don't have to do anything.
Just lie there and pretend you are dead."

Karie McNeley

Maternal Bait and Switch

Women love babies.
Dressing them.
Feeding them on occasion.
Changing them...maybe.
Putting them in the crib.
Ditching them in a high chair for a few hours
while they go out for a few beers.

But what women love more than babies
are other women's babies.
Playing with them.
Laughing with them.
Singing with them.
And telling their friends
how they wish their own children
were just as smart.

Meg Eden

Reunion

Forty years later, my mother sees
her high school history teacher
at the entrance of Borders.

The woman looks over my mother
with her black stretch pants, orange-
blonde hair (from the rust in our well water),
sagging and blotched cheeks,

and rubs my mother's shoulders
as if comforting a widow when she says,
*And we always thought
you'd grow up to be Miss America.*

For the rest of the day, my mother
smiles and reminds herself, *I could
have been Miss America.*

I grab my heavy hips in my hands,
wishing I'd had a similar chance.

Elmast Kozloyan

The first and possibly last poem
I will ever write on this matter

She chiseled away at her nose
The one that looked like her mother's did
before she too hacked it away
They had fled to the other side of the world
and built a nest with expensive shiny things
They fled when their people were sent into deserts
Marching to their grave stones
When babies were thrown into the Black Sea
or poisoned with toxic gas in school houses
Never given the chance to pass down the broad noses
their parents gave them

I saw my history in tiny cups
stained with black ink coffee
While she kept checking the mirror
just to make sure it hadn't grown back
I didn't recognize her anymore
Hers wasn't the face I had grown up with
It was left behind with those who starved
as the Reds patted themselves on the back for their glorious union

My grandmother would tell me how beautiful I was
but if I got a nose job
how much prettier I would be
I felt sorry for her
That she would go her entire life without
seeing anything past her own vanity
I still love her even if she will never understand why
I'll never shrink my nose
lift my breasts
or freeze my face
and I will never understand why
she is so ashamed of the face her son gave me

Daryna Barykina

Behind the Bruised Mask

Ashley M. Jones

What It Means To Say Sally Hemings

Bright Girl Sally
Mulatto Sally
Well Dressed Sally
Sally With the Pretty Hair
Sally With the Irish Cotton Dress
Sally With the Smallpox Vaccine
Sally, Smelling of Clean White Soap
Sally Never Farmed A Day In Her Life
Available Sally
Nursemaid Sally
Sally, Filled with Milk
Sally Gone to Paris with Master's Daughter
Sally in the Chamber with the President
Sally in the Chamber with the President's Brother
Illiterate Sally
Capable Sally
Unmarried Sally
Sally, Mother of Madison, Harriet, Beverly, Eston
Sally, Mother of Eston Who Changed His Name
Sally, Mother of Eston Hemings Jefferson
Eston, Who Made Cabinets
Eston, Who Made Music
Eston, Who Moved to Wisconsin
Eston, Whose Children Were Jeffersons
Eston, Who Died A White Man
Grandmother Sally of the White Hemingses
Infamous Sally
Silent Sally
Sally, Kept at Monticello Until Jefferson's Death
Sally, Whose Children Were Freed Without Her

LeAnne Hunt

Advice to My Daughter on How to Navigate Hellfire Damnation and the Arctic Circle

In the future, someone may call you hot,
but remember
some children are attracted to fire. They call
flames pretty but stomp them out when
playtime is over.
Don't be the ash under anyone's feet,
but don't burn anyone just to see the smoke.
If you refuse to light up for a lover,
you may be called frigid. But you know
that ice melts if held long enough
in a palm or mouth.
If you choose to share your warmth,
people may call you other names.
People call girls names for either yes
or no, and boys only for a no.
Virginity is not a prize but a space for
possibilities.
It is the line in the sand that you rub away,
but the sand remains.
If the body is a temple, the heart is a votive.
Let yours shine.

Sage

Mara Buck

In defiance of J. Alfred...

I grow old and
I eat many peaches.

Bring on your beaches—
I shall walk them

With unrolled trousers
Wet with spray and salt.

I have no need of mermaids
Nor lamplight nor soft brown hair.

I am the woman talking
To myself of Michelangelo.

Jackie Joice
Cuban Lady with a Cigar

Kim Dower

Boob Job

Trying on clothes in the backroom
of Loehmann's, a stranger invites me
to feel her breasts, a stranger trying on
dresses that don't fit and I can see
her breasts are larger than they want
to be, and she can see I'm watching,
asks me to help zip her up and I struggle
to pull her in, smooth out her sunburned skin,
tug, ask her to shake herself in, she tells me
she just got them, didn't know they'd come out
so big isn't sure she likes them, not even her
husband cares, he's not a breast man, she says,
he's an ass man *but I'm not getting an ass job,*
good, I say, because how do you even *get* an ass job,
do you want to feel them, she asks, and I do, so I do
and they feel like bean bags you'd toss at a clown's face
at a kid's party, I squeeze them both at the same time,
cup my hands underneath them, she says, *go ahead,*
squeeze some more, it's not sexual, aren't they heavy,
I don't want to have them around every day, her nipples
headlights staring into the dressing room mirror, red scars
around their circumferences, angry circles I want to run
my finger around, *you should have seen them before*
I had them lifted, they were long drooping points,
couldn't stand looking at them anymore, can I see yours,
so I show her, so small hers could eat mine alive,
nipples like walnuts, do you think I should make mine
bigger, and there we are examining one another's boobs,
touching, talking about them like they aren't there,
don't matter, forgetting how it felt when we were twelve
or thirteen, one morning when they first appeared
sore, swollen, exciting, new, when they had the power
to turn us into women we no longer knew.

Angelita Ortega
A Tease and a Toast

Sarah Thursday

Some Haphazard Line Tied
onto a Kitchen Table

Be here. Be centered. Be a girl on the verge of everything.
Be the wrong kind of naive. Be the wrong kind of experienced.
Be nestled in pine bench seats. Be as bright as fluorescent bulbs.
Be a mother cooking spaghetti. Be ducks in blue flower tiles.
Be a wall telephone, spiral cord stretched for miles. Be a
pimpled-faced teen. Be a former homeless child sleeping
in her own room. Be dancing on clean white sparkled
linoleum. Be a shy step-daughter. Be a visiting sister
towing another man behind. Be glass tabletop,
chipped edges for all night D&D. Be a pile of
endless dishes. Be cooking sherry snuck by
seventeen-year-olds. Be cartoons. Be drawn
on the refrigerator door. Be gaping windows.
Be a kind of glue. Be her best memories.

Leigh Ann Hornfeldt

Poem for T

We've exhausted the alphabet, wrung phrases
dry. Made new ones when the old ones

wouldn't do. 129 miles of coax cable
have delivered my small miseries to your inbox,

carried your consolations back to the cell phone
I hold instead of your hand.

I know your shoe size, your bourbon.
That once you searched all afternoon

for the right pair of Kelly green skinny jeans,
stayed awake to watch for meteors

after I'd fallen asleep. You've scratched out
my rage with your fingernails,

shared the gloom of horoscopes,
tarots, an old psychic. Leo, we've howled

and burnt dinner in the kitchen.
We've cleared calendars, set aside years, spit in our palms,

held on tight. Roared through the wrong men.
We've passed revolution back and forth like a love note during class.

Kathryn Pellman

Tea for One

Joan Jobe Smith

What I Learned from the Movies

When I hear shocking news, I will faint.
When my fiance leaves me holding a candlestick on the haunted house
staircase to go for help 20 miles away, the vampire will bite my neck.
When my fiance and the bad guy begin to fight over the nitroglycerin/
uranium or something that will destroy every living thing on earth if
spilled, I will hit on the head with a Ming vase, baseball bat or Maltese
falcon—my fiance. When the handsome singing cowboy who saved my
life and my father's ranch from the dastard banker or Apaches kisses me
and rides off into the horizon on his white horse, I will smile and disappear.
When I am in the family way and ride a horse or walk down stairs, I will
fall and lose the child I am carrying. When my child coughs or sneezes,
he/she will die. When my child dies, my husband will blame me and I will
take to streetwalking and drinking whisky with stevedores along the wharf,
lose my looks and will to live and throw myself beneath the wheels of a
locomotive or a black La Salle sedan. When a telegram arrives, it will
always tell me that my fiance has died in the war. When the moon is
full, a man will either kiss me or kill me. When I wear marabou and
contemplate suicide while gazing at the Manhattan skyline, Fred Astaire
will ask me to dance. When Elvis tries to kiss me on the balcony, a gang
of girls will ask him to sing while they push me over the railing into a
swimming pool. When Marilyn Monroe is near, I will suddenly bear a
striking resemblance to a bean and egg burrito. When I am 40 like Blanche
Dubois, yet still have smooth crème fraiche skin, I will place paper lanterns
over light bulbs of desire to hide my aging face to spare young men from
shrinking from the hideousness of my old woman-ness and when I am 50
like Norma Desmond, even though I still have skin as smooth as cream
cheese, I will beg for a close-up so's to terrify every man on earth with my
antiquity and when I am 70 or more and must scrub floors to earn a living, I
will work on my hands and knees with rags and buckets while the men use
mops and smoke cigars. And: when I cry Oh! and they call for a doctor and
he tells them to boil water, I will die.

Amanda Rochelle Martin

Venus Envy

Even on my knees,
I can make a man
praise the God he
swears he doesn't
believe in. I want
to tell him that
God is Me.

Amanda Rochelle Martin

Moon in Capricorn

Lee Kottner

Statuesque

Neither Rubens nor Botticelli
would look twice at her.

Yet, discontent
with a body so comfortable
in the provocative,
she lies rigid on her hard bed
willing her flesh
to transmogrify
into the real substance
of all those Norman tombs
in her past.
Despairing of it, she wails
It moves!
as though it should cling to her bones
in a solid mass
like marble or bronze, not
the assemblage of meat and gristle
it is.
She walks miles each day
as though to outdistance
her body, leave
its quivering muscles,
gravity-afflicted pockets of fat,
its treacherous revealing skin
behind,
as though motion and sweat alone
will release her
from its disappointments
and she will solidify,
harden,
and, this achieved,
become her own pedestal.

Sarah Wheatley

Earrings

I can't remember deciding to be a boy. I can remember sitting under a bush, mustering the courage to ask the girls if I could play with them; I can remember one of them saying, "OK. Step in that hole there. Oh poor kitty, you drowned. OK, you played, and you died. Go away." I can remember playing kickball with the boys on a windy, wet day, sliding into home and getting covered in mud. Paul pulled me to my feet and Nigel gave me a high five. It was natural selection, driven by the icy winds, barren deserts, and sweet cedar tree-forts of the feral nature of children. It was evolution.

I refused to wear the beautiful Laura Ingalls Wilder dresses my mom gave me. I put my doll away, a relic of "When I was little." I violently resisted wearing a dress for a violin recital. My best friend re-taught me to ride a bike (contrary to popular belief, it is possible to forget). In our overalls, we rode bikes, baked cookies, dammed ditches, played Harry Potter, and explored the woods behind her house. Walks home from school were spent discussing *Lord of the Rings*, or in cattail, mud, snowball, or blackberry fights. Somebody told me if I could kiss my elbow I'd turn into a boy, and I nearly dislocated my shoulder trying. I read *Rascal, My Dog Skip*, and *My Side of the Mountain* over and over, trying to re-create those boys' idyllic childhoods in my own scrappy but beautiful clear-cuts on Galbraith Mountain. All in all, it was a darn good life for a not-quite-boy.

But there were still places where I was unwelcome, no matter how hard I worked. Paintball, for instance, and the most hardcore and enviable of outdoor adventures. My brother's Boy Scout troop got to go on a 175-mile canoe trip and snow camping at Mt. Baker. The way I had it figured, boys got to learn to survive outdoors, build things, and fix things—useful skills. Girls got cooking and knitting—also useful skills—but there were a lot of stupid skills aimed at pleasing boys too, like makeup, which consumed a lot of time. Most of all, it seemed that boys and men asked for what they wanted and got it. If one had to be a boy to do those things, well, bras and such be damned, I would.

I refused to get in the car for weeks, riding my bike everywhere as soon as I fought my way into the right to bike alone. I made a New Year's resolution to not cry for a whole year between twelve and thirteen, and I did it, except for two tears at the end of *Bridge to Terabithia* (and nobody saw those). I went to Girl Scout camp and reveled in boats, hiking, swimming, fire building, and camp craft skills (though never as long or as hardcore as my younger brother's Boy Scout adventures). I idolized my teenage counselors, women who did those things, but I still thought of them as "boy" things. I grew up and worked at camp, teaching girls those same skills. I didn't understand more than the mechanics of what I was doing, though I did feel a sense of triumph for campers who overcame their fears of swim checks or snakes—as if my side was one little girl closer to winning.

The spring I was twenty-four, I was the teaching assistant for a field-based natural history course at my university. The rest of the teaching staff was all men, but kind men, men who have never made me feel even the least bit different for being female. I wasn't even thinking about being the only woman on the teaching team.

On our trip to Santa Cruz Island, the women in the class came to me, first one, then another, then another. Quietly, hesitantly at first, they asked me questions whose answers could not be found in nature or in the Jepson Manual of Higher Plants of California. How do I take a woman's role in natural history? one wondered. What does that mean? Is there a place for women in natural history, a place with more creativity, art, stewardship, tending, responsibility? Perhaps with less competition as to who has seen the most birds? I feel stifled, angry, no, fighting mad, furious, at the arrogance of one particular boy, another woman said; how can we make him shut up and consider for a moment what it might be like to not have everything handed to you?!

I did not know the answers to these questions, not at first. I had never considered what a woman's role in natural history might be. I had considered my role—a lover of botany, farming, teaching, and ducks—I had contemplated my role as an incredibly fortunate modern human in the ecosystems I inhabit, but I had never imagined my gender as part of it.

Those questions were birds singing of truth outside my window. That spring, I woke up and realized that as a woman who studies nature, not only do I have access to the still male-dominated world of science, I have the power and responsibility of being a bridge. I looked back at Girl Scout camp and realized how many women had invited me into that world, alongside my pushing to be included among men. I saw myself as one of them and saw that that mattered. I was humbled and proud, but mostly humbled by the great privilege and luck I've had as far as supportive people and beautiful places are concerned. I saw the great weaselly subtlety of the ways girls are encouraged to leave dirt and leaves and birds behind, and realized that I'd come through by refusing to see those million small mechanisms of discouragement. I don't think ignoring them is a bad way to go. We live in a country where we can do that. But there are people who can't, and it is for them that I stand under a tree with a hand lens, heart open, ready to teach and learn with anyone who agrees to give a shit.

I went home from that trip to Santa Cruz Island and asked my housemate Kira to pierce my ears. I wanted something to remind me, every time I looked in the mirror, to see a woman alongside the nature-marks, messy hair and scars that form my identity. To remind me so that I remember: What you love does not depend on what's in your pants, and it's my job not only to give myself that acknowledgement, but to teach it to others. Not only is it possible to be a woman and love what I love, it's necessary.

Kira gave me a shot of tequila and a piece of ice, poked borrowed sharp earrings through my ears, and I went back into the kitchen. "What, you did it? You didn't even make any noise!" said the boys. "What did you expect?" I asked, grinning. Some battles aren't won in a day, and to teach requires humor and patience.

My students made me my first earrings at the end of the quarter—white alder cones they'd collected on a slender silver wire. Their alder seeds are spent, but they hold other seeds: tolerance, patience, humility, power, responsibility. Though they weigh nothing, they make my back stronger and my shoulders broader.

For Kate, Amy, Emily, Kayla, Rachel, Dora, Nadia and Justine, the truth-birds

Sandra Ramos O'Briant

Crispy Feminist Flan Cake:

½ cup sexist daddy
1 cup manipulative Mexican mommy
¼ cup domineering grandmother
2 cups fiction, fantasy, and lies
¼ tsp. poor impulse control (risk-taking can be substituted)
A dash of pachucas beating the crap out of you
Mix in Texan/New Mexican racism
Add 60's protests
Add drugs and sex to taste
Toss in a sugar daddy
Sprinkle with Santa Fe art and bake in the sun
        blazing down on the Sangre de Cristos.

It's ready when the center springs back no matter how many times it's punched
Let it cool while watched by benevolent lesbians, compassionate crones,
        and loving sons
Keep it in the fortress of its baking dish
Your reward will be a creamy tartsweet dessert
        edged with hard-won brown crisp.

Amanda Rochelle Martin

R.I.P. Being Needy

Sarah Thursday

Unknown Employee

I saw a girl at Target, she was me
at twenty-one years old.
She had my blond hair

and simple black-lined eyes,
a red vest and black band shirt
from Joy Division's Unknown

Pleasures. Iconic jagged white
mountain lines I once
plastered to my purse.

The image is a badge, I know
immediately, she is cool
in the way I was cool

working at Target at twenty-one.
I want to tell her we got bigger
plans, even if you can't see it now,

and that boy, who torments your soul,
is just passing by. I want to tell her
we end up alright, and all that confusion

might not get clear,
but it settles. And all that sadness,
the endless sadness fades away,

but I give her a slight grin
and muster, "I like your shirt."
I don't know how else to say it,

so I pay and leave for home.

NEEDY

ARM

143

Elaine Mintzer

Stigma

Girls are given names that encourage self-control,
good manners and sunny dispositions:
Rose.
Lily.
Names that speak of ancestral landscapes
and fragrance:
Heather.
Jasmine.
Even Iris, for our sexual proclivities
and our mothers' desires that we grow beautiful
but not wild.
Never Dandelion.
Never Clover.

My mother called me Margarita,
an optimistic name for a daisy
that grows abundantly in containers
sacrificing everything for a short bloom
before it falls to the cement, spent.

My lover checks out a new neighbor in shorts
as she pulls two panting beagles on tight leashes.
"Look at the bougainvillea,"
he tells me as his eyes linger on her legs,
"the way the petals fade clear and papery."

I am transparent with this lack of attention.
I want his eye and his hand,
not the name of our relationship.
Under my lacy dress, I swear
I'm as wild as the weeds beneath his feet.

When I have daughters,
I will name them after stones:

Obsidian.
Granite.
Or for metals impervious to rust and decay:
Chromium.
Cobalt.
Nothing quiet or easy to ignore.
I will call them Lightning and Thunder.
Freedom.
Swift Bird of Prey.
Right Here Right Now.

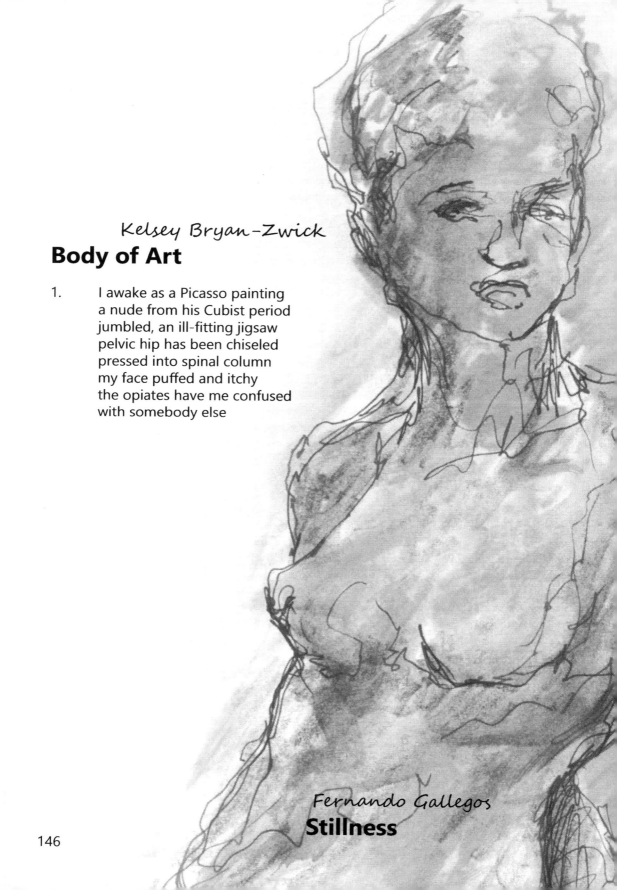

Kelsey Bryan-Zwick

Body of Art

1. I awake as a Picasso painting
    a nude from his Cubist period
    jumbled, an ill-fitting jigsaw
    pelvic hip has been chiseled
    pressed into spinal column
    my face puffed and itchy
    the opiates have me confused
    with somebody else

Fernando Gallegos
Stillness

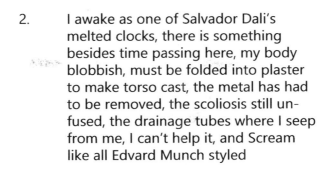

2.   I awake as one of Salvador Dali's
melted clocks, there is something
besides time passing here, my body
blobbish, must be folded into plaster
to make torso cast, the metal has had
to be removed, the scoliosis still un-
fused, the drainage tubes where I seep
from me, I can't help it, and Scream
like all Edvard Munch styled

3.   I awake as Frida Kahlo's self-portrait
my broken back, her broken back
the dream seems to become more real
tugs at the at the peripherals, images
superimposed, a pattern shapes motif
a picture of life, stills, comes into focus

4.   I awake as a Grecian statue
ancient busted-bust, the shoulder
blade, ribs, left thigh, have gone
numb, covered in dust, in the rubble
sheets draped like a toga
I eat my grape Jell-O, adjust
the bed, recline towards relief

5.   I awake as the Bride of Frankenstein's
Monster's doppelgänger, the screws
in my neck tighten as the clouds are
about to gather, my movements
static, wires connected to me beep
in the electric machine, my eyes turn
green when lightning strikes

6.   I awake as the Bionic Woman
or the cost of pale and sickly
has me looking like a million bucks
and really this is my fortune
to experience art as canvas or
great slab of stone, to be sculpted
scalpeled, painted with iodine
combined with rare metals, gilded
this body worth its weight and
worthwhile, gold and golden

Kirsten Clodfelter

Because Misogyny

Because misogyny: Elliot Rodger.

Because misogyny: Every man Elliot Rodger calls to mind. Every man who has let the whistled catcall of *hot momma* morph in his mouth to *stuck-up bitch* when that tried-and-true method of objectifying a complete stranger fails to get him laid. Every man who has complained of being friend-zoned as if the act of being decent—as if simply treating a woman like a human being—is all it could take.

Because misogyny: Equality as radical. Empowerment as weapon. Feminist as feminazi. At some point, doesn't a history of domestic violence, of rape, of murder, of torture, of withholding count as its own Holocaust? The terror George W. hunted to finally justify a war?

Because misogyny: Filmmakers Woody Allen and Roman Polanski are lionized as their own type of victim. Misunderstood. Brilliance over ethics. Over empathy. Art as disassociation. As inculpable. Steubenville mourns ruined football careers. *Playboy* lauds Neko Case only as a woman in music.

Because misogyny: A talented, well-meaning poet attempts to process trauma through art and gifts a new voice to the wrong protagonist of this story.

Because misogyny: A friend posts an article on Isla Vista and someone comments, "Come on, ladies, take one for the team," as if women weren't just murdered over a man's sense of entitlement. Have ever been murdered over a man's sense of entitlement. As if a person's right to humor of course trumps a person's right to safety. To comfort. But actually, not really *person*. Woman.

Because misogyny: A comedian co-opts #YesAllWomen at our expense without bothering to be subversive or challenging or even funny. When the jokes fall flat, are returned in echo, these men recoil at the thought of reflection, rush to fill the silence with their own extraordinary reasoning, take solace in their certainty that they are the exception, never the rule.

Because misogyny: An older male colleague whose name I don't know finds me in an adjunct office one afternoon, my belly ripe and low-hanging and nearly ready for the picking as I organize papers before class. He takes a long look at my ring finger—bare—before he asks, *Is the father in the picture?* I am too stunned to smile, to extend my hand for a strong shaking, to chirp through my teeth that, where I come from, which is anywhere, we usually start with *hello*. Instead I choke the yes from my throat to his brightening. *That's good*—the balloon of relief inflated almost to bursting, as if the whole of my daughter's personhood, her very legitimacy, is tied to this. As if there is nothing worse he could imagine for my child than the thought of me raising her alone.

Because misogyny: My gentle father comes to visit and still occasionally says things like, *Sometimes you just have to shut up and let a woman pick the curtains,* like there is one secret, and this is it. Nevermind that in our cramped apartment, curtains are a luxury. Nevermind that a blanket —gifted to me a decade ago for my high school graduation—hangs covering our daughter's bedroom window. Nevermind that it's my partner, the dad, who most often fixes our toddler's hair; who is the best at picking out cute, coordinated outfits; who successfully executes DIY Pinterest projects while my own crafting attempts disintegrate into unrecognizable piles of hot glue and yarn.

Because misogyny: That my partner does these things for our daughter —that he makes pancakes good enough to put your favorite hole-in-the-wall diner breakfast to shame, that he doesn't hesitate to run the vacuum, that he asks my opinion and considers my feelings in front of others— sometimes earns him less-than-favorable labels. *Whipped. Weak. Pussy.* Because that's the greatest insult we can think of: To tell a man he's acting like the lesser sex—like a fucking woman.

Because misogyny: Men who meet the minimum expectation of how to treat other people—any gender—feel charged to speak up *for themselves* when these daily injustices finally grow into too heavy a burden for us to carry quietly, as if it's they who are oppressed, rushing to remind us it's #NotAllMen because it's easier when there's distance, easier to step back or away than to lean in, easier to act as aggressor than ally.

Because misogyny: I've heard, *But he was drunk*, as if it was an absolution.

Because misogyny: I've heard, *But she was drunk*, as if it was an absolution.

Because misogyny: Before there was a sweet baby or a partner who lifts me up with his kindness, a man who was once my husband felt entitled to hide our car keys or laptop from me during arguments. To throw dishes or destroy my things as if this was a fair compromise for keeping his hands off of me. As if there was still so much for which I should have been grateful. Finally our friends felt called forward to share—with concern, hesitation—that from the mouth of the man who had vowed his love, and always, I was *a worthless waste of space, dumb, a child*. This entitlement is pervasive, endemic, impossible to escape. So many instances that there isn't enough time or space to name even the smallest fraction. So many that my own barely make a dent. Are hardly worth blinking an eye over.

Because misogyny: A mutual friend once visited in the middle of the day and told me to pack a bag and come with her, worried that I was no longer safe living with the husband. Of escalation. Days later, she explained that his mother—a woman I both trusted and adored—had sat in my kitchen and listened to the charge of *verbally and emotionally abusive* and then waited until I'd left the room to whisper her own solution: I needed to *grow up*, to *stop acting like such a baby*. C'mon, ladies. Take one for the team.

But I won't.

Chelsea Krob
Split

Keayva Mitchell

To The Ones Who Question Proper

Learn to swallow pearls. Swallow them whole. Unstring them first if you're a beginner. It may not seem like it but eventually a trachea learns to quit raging against the pearly snake down. Don't bite. Let the smooth gloss of them ease down the pink brick road of your mouth. Or, if you're a biter, make sure to avoid salt afterwards as it might aggravate gum shards. Let your mother shine a pen light, the one she got from the bank, behind your molars and beneath your tongue after each one. If not your mother, then an aunt, or a close friend, or a stranger will do. If not a pen light, then a keen eye, a pointed finger, a glob of spit will do. Make sure your throat is luminescent. Make sure your mouth is always pink.

Examine your jewel-filled body. There is a certain luster that sets in with time. Revel in your new skin. Blink with new eyes. Spread new fingers until the webs of your hands ache. Discover the new things your hands can do. Hold other hands, untangle knots, write letters, pull people in, push people away. Learn to love your hands but nothing else. Believe you are more like the sea than the sea because you are bursting with its treasures. Drown yourself in blue. Blue is okay because it's something like sadness and all the greats wore it. Submerge yourself just deep enough that you become something mystical. If not become, then look like will do. If not look like then pretend will do. Emerge dripping lonely and wet and hypothermic.

Open yourself up like an old wallet. Use your fingernails to scratch out the dust between Velcro seams. Let your precious things clatter out and roll around. Find yourself in bathroom scrawls and behind locked doors. Beneath blaring Journey songs in basements you can't adequately describe. Discover nipples and knees and in between places in the folds. Discover shadows. Realize when they say pearl sometimes it only means a transaction of mouth to mouth. Let the world oyster-ride you. Listen to sad songs. Remember when your ears felt brand new. Realize songs are only as sad as the person hearing them. Listen anyways. Find a blurry pearl on a barroom floor. Take it twice. Don't bite. If not a pearl, a lover will do. If not a lover, a stranger will do. Swallow them whole. Or, if you're a biter, bite gently. It may not seem like it at first but eventually a trachea learns to quit raging against. Make sure it recollects its luminescence. Remember that your mouth has always been soft pink and pearl-scarred. Ask your mouth what pain is. It knows. It knows.

Dana Anastasia
Forgetting Form

I forget my own breasts,
slumped like tired dogs
across my chest.

I think of the hands
that have held them,
mouths that have bit
and flicked them

and I find myself wishing
that everyone else
would forget them, too.

Melissa Dale
Marine

Mara Buck

No way...

I have never dreamt of flowing dresses,

trains to trip me up,
veils to blind me,

elaborate fingernails to cripple my hands
as I tear off false lashes,

silicon and Botox and
Spanx and Panx and the obligatory arsenal

to create of *Me* the *She* of the
airbrushed illusion.

I am not Marie Antoinette,
though I like my cake.

We shall share it
and grow fat and happy
together.

Keep your ankle-spraining stilettos,
your push-up bras,

your murderous pantyhose and
all the powder and the paint,

for I am the female of the species
who had the sense to eat the apple

and I found it most delicious.

Christina Elaine Vasquez

Mother's Perfume

Being born a woman comes with so many strings attached, strings that can bind us to the roles we are told we must play and blind us to how much we are capable of. There's a reason we have been kept in our place for so many centuries. Society has never liked to look the vagina in the eye. There is too much truth there. While the penis is celebrated, the open vagina is illusive and unpainted, closed off only to be found in the underground of all-nude strip clubs, pornos and magazines so that some can gaze upon its perplexity of pleasure. It is not tidy like a cock. Its folds and creases make it wonderfully mysterious and complicated. It is the cycle of life and death, the source of incredible pain as well as bliss. It is the origins of man! Divinity in the flesh! Nature remembers the power of the feminine. It is painted with blood on the lips of its cunning huntresses and fierce mother protectors. It is our cages that have made us forget. We have the capability to shape society by shaping our creations—to respect and love. I adore my vagina. I even like the smell, it reminds me of chicken noodle soup. I sometimes sit and take in the aroma like an animal. I think about how funny it would be to suffocate the faces of oppression with it, placing labia over all airways until they cease to exist. The world's enemies never respect the vagina. What an ironic end that would be, to be smothered by the "world" you have no respect for, while she screams, "I have endured rape, battery, suppression, conditioning. I can bleed for days, but I will no longer bleed for you!" Such a proper death of Tyranny to sit unladylike on his face.

BC Petrakos

the best women

I saw the best women of my generation
buckle down and lose their sense of humor
get fat, and make children in the midwest
under financial impossibilities

I saw the best women of my generation
tormented by financial insecurities
      the money haunts
      the money taunts
the partner wishes we were something else
and we are—we really are something else

I saw the best women of my generation
put down their paintbrushes,
microphones, guitars and acting resumes

I saw the best women of my generation
slip into sheets with other women
just to have a good dose of orgasmic oral
without complaint or strings attached

I saw the best women of my generation
cry for men who in their middle age
wander to barflies' beds and feed children
who are not their own, not looking back

I was there, I saw—
good women gutted like fish
because they loved and loved
and got nothing in return

I saw the best women of my generation
shut down their sexual desires knowing
that the ring on a finger, and their name on a lease
meant a hostage situation, that whiskey is the answer
to love gone dry, that a lonely headache
in the middle of the night meant one more trip
to the pharmacy for that pill, a substitute for intimacy

I was there—I saw her leave her husband
for a younger man, just for the younger man
to say goodbye once he got on his feet

I was there—I saw her work two jobs
and put him though higher education
just to have him split with a younger version
of herself—one with a "positive attitude"
one who didn't have to do without for years
one who was "put together" and not
tired all the time—smiling in anticipation

I saw the best women of my generation
used over and over again like handiwipes
needing to be thrown away

I was there—
I saw the best women of my generation
for the sake of loneliness take on men
who wouldn't work and cheated and used
their fists to show they cared

I was there—
I saw the best women of my generation
stood up against the wall
and shot down
because they had the nerve
to age and work and love and exist—

THIS is the reason to howl
the reason to howl
a reason to howl

Toti O'Brien
Lebimbe

Mark A. Fisher

Bletchley Park

75%
that's right
75%
of the famed code-breaking house
were Wrens
women
that each night deciphered
codes
saved lives
and shortened the war
then for years after
had their lives
their service
declared secret
hidden like their intelligence
behind laundry and cooking
proper feminine deference
to real heroes
that couldn't have done it
without them

Esmeralda Villalobos
**Observa, crea y expande
tus sentidos like a girl.**

Sarah Lilius

War for Dinner

after "Photograph of the Girl," Sharon Olds

War is redefined
as the city breaks.
Death is a news flash.
Destruction, a televised event.

The privileged
flip and pan.
Loose propaganda is gold
they recite at dinner.

Here: young girls shift
and reach for less food across
the dinner table. The men
argue and the boys kick.

There: young girls hide under tables,
cradle their knees, rock fast
against splitting cement. The men
fall dead and the boys run.

Soldiers with foreign tongue
circle the city—fast vultures,
instinct blackened.
Boots crackle shattered window.

There: the city cramps, presses
young wombs ready.
The young girls brink, they pass
over without their mothers.

Here: the young girls bleed
on satin cushions.
They excuse themselves and shame
is passed by their mothers like a dish.

Keayva Mitchell

sidewalk bird, unwritten

by ruined I meant how she can be the wispy half form
of white clouds on sunny days shapeless lovely drift
and by ruffled I meant the way she feels angry sometimes
to walk like a woman and talk like a woman and only
get just enough decompose how the lyrics fall right out of
her matter when she's happy and some days she wants to be
stretched elbow akimbo knee flying flying but it's not fitting
without being wasted without wanting the wrecked figure
and sometimes she wants to be recognized by her breasts and
in spite of them her jewelry wasn't stolen she just can't afford
any yet or maybe someone left her and sometimes the memories
are crows pecking at her skull and sometimes it hits something like
 tiny but inevitable but she's picked herself up swept herself
into place who's to say all of her everything is not the sway
of her hips the arch lift of her neck breaking men's backs leaving
them pavement trampled concrete crushed as she walks by
like she don't feel much like flying today.

Debbie J Cho

Rachel

Ricki Mandeville

The Wait

Ten years old and waiting for my breasts,
sideways to the mirror half a dozen
times a day, examining by lamplight
my pale chest, flat as any schoolboy's.

While my parents lay asleep,
I'd vision myself
burgeoning round and womanly,
the stares of boys as I glided
past them in my pink cashmere sweater
and one day a man's hand, perfect and gentle
cupping my grown curves as I had seen—
just for an instant, passing the doorway—
my father's hand
mold my mother's breast from behind
as she stood at the sink washing dishes:
my father's indrawn breath,
my mother's eyes closing,
her hands suddenly still in the suds.

How simple to lay out my notions
of womanhood like shimmering fairy tiles
along the white slopes of the breasts
I would sprout like luscious fruits,
wear like badges, flaunt like bait,
luring attention, desire, true love.

How naïve not to notice the woman
down the street, and the women downtown
working day jobs and night shifts
with their lovely breasts and lined foreheads
and tired faces and aching feet
and too many children
and no man.

How silly to miss, floating
somewhere beyond my comprehension,
nearly invisible in the dazzle of my ripening,
the blood, the burden, the weariness, the pain.

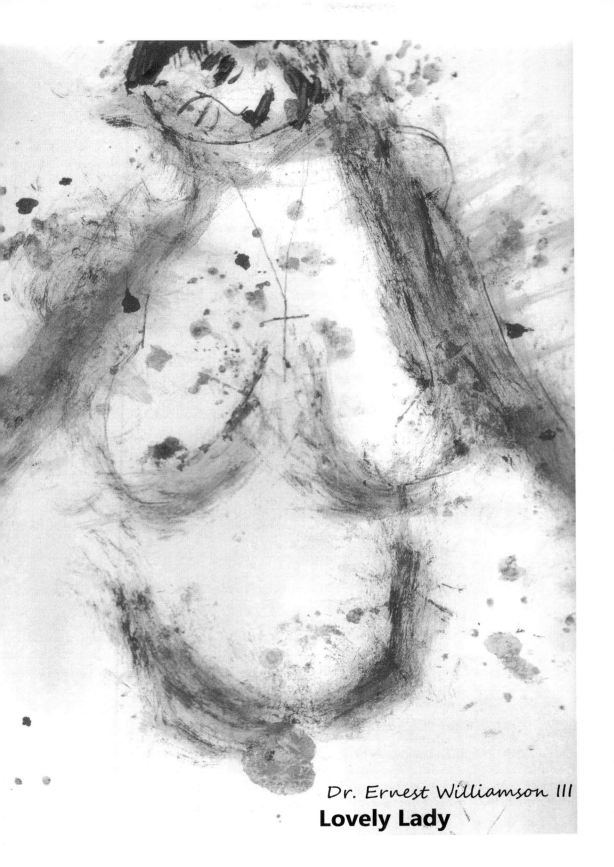

Dr. Ernest Williamson III
Lovely Lady

Carmel Reid Mawle

Owls

Huddled in our Alaskan snow cave, my third grade compadres and I decided we needed secret nicknames. We'd built a rough igloo out of clumps from the snow plough mountain, with two lumpy snow-benches, a snow-table, and a porthole to track the playground lady. Add a forbidden candle, matches stolen from Cheryl's brother, and we were Lake Otis Elementary outlaws. Of course we needed code names.

We decided on Winnie-the-Pooh names, because we were all fans, though none of us wanted the bear's name with its unmentionable double entendre. Cheryl, whose mom still curled her hair into baby-ish Shirley Temple coils, became Roo; Cathy, orange-headed and belt stripes across her back, Tigger. I became Owl for my quiet wisdom (a common misconception about the shy), and was designated the club counselor. I took the position seriously because my club mates brought real problems. They appreciated the scheming quality of my solutions – something akin to Walt Disney's *Parent Trap,* but without the happy endings. When Roo interrupted her parents' late-night screaming match by asking for a drink of water, her dad stormed out of the house. When Tigger buried her dad's belt in the snow, he used his hand. I had my own problems – a babysitter who forced lead-based paint, toilet water, and stinky body parts into my mouth, but I didn't discuss these things in our group. Owl was meant to have the answers, not questions.

We never considered going to an adult for help. Grown-ups were the enemy tribe. I'd learned that lesson the year before when my parents found a note hinting of my after-school hell; the shaming hurt worse than the spanking. Instead, our plans grew more elaborate. We lit our candle in the cold white cave, and devised foggy-breathed schemes involving stolen car keys, nests of yellow jackets, and escaped zoo animals. We leaned our hooded heads together, and giggled through moist knit scarves and wolf fur trim. There was warmth in the illusion of control.

After fourth grade, my family moved from town to a narrow strip of development on a dirt road beneath Flat Top Mountain. It was late afternoon, deep winter, sky black and glittering. I walked the snow-packed road home through a hushed forest of hoar-frosted birch and stunted mountain hemlocks, snow-laden and slumping heavily against each other. Branches thick with white crystals and mounds of snow, all shades of brilliant white, reflected every twinkle of starlight. I walked with mittened hands pushed deep into the pockets of down parka, the only sound my billowing white breath, and the rhythmic crunch of wafflestompers on frozen tire tread.

Until the sacred reverberation of icy air carved open by wings – and two great white snowy owls lighted in the frozen birch beside me. White, on white, on white, and four bright gold eyes blinking. They were close enough that I could have reached out and touched their feathered bodies. I stood breathing in the sparkling silence, blinking back, my toes and fingers and cheeks growing hot with numbness.

A simple shape – two pointed ears, concave circles for eyes, wedged grooves hinting at wings. Cupped in my eleven-year-old palm, the owl was cool to the touch, but quickly absorbed the heat of my hand, as if life surged warm beneath the surface of the soft stone. Still weary of the grown-up tribe, their treacherous ways and fickle notice, the gift from my teacher was unexpected. He'd carved it himself from deep ochre soapstone, speckled through with black and rust, and polished it to a shine – a going-away present.

My dad had taken up with the pretty next-door neighbor who sewed psychedelic halter dresses and painted pet rocks. She was divorcing her husband, presumably because too much carrot juice had colored the whites of his eyes. The five of us kids would be scattered like dandelion fluff, and I would be swept from the Alaskan wilderness and the solace of stories spun from moss-covered rooms damp with buried streams, cathedral ceilings of leafy branches, and chick-a-dee choirs.

Forty years later, the sculpture sits beneath a lamp on my desk, its wing chipped by a grandson's enthusiastic admiration. I think of its creator often, his folk guitar and scraggly beard, and how he pretended not to notice when I only mouthed the words to our school program. He read my stories aloud to my classmates, because I could not find the voice, but I had never told him about my snow cave nickname, or the great whites who blessed me on a winter's afternoon. Mr. Eaton was a grown-up who looked, not for what he could take from this child, nor for what she might take from him; he looked, and saw, and then he pulled a small creature from deep within a stone. This owl was a kindness.

Denise R. Weuve

Rain

for Yvonne Sham-Shackleton

Since you returned home,
it has rained once or twice,
hard petal-like drops
scrubbing the streets clean
of oil leaks and old leaves.
In my back yard, the hopscotch frame
is gone as well, those purple squares
we drew with my niece's thumb-thick chalk,
disappeared as if we never called turns,
tossed nickel markers, or pirouetted
in 180-degree twirls.
        For a moment
we were nine, did not bother
with make-up to entice boys,
let our ponytails bounce,
believed that the pink plastic heart-
shaped rings were wedding bands
encircling us to each other
through knee scrapes,
Chinese jump ropes,
and roughed-up rag dolls;
a closeness husbands cannot touch.

Alice Kociemba

Qui est la plus belle?

I'm the silver backing—
the mirror's memory
that reflects your image
and holds your essence.
I love the entirety of you.

I have seen you crawl over,
pull yourself up, clap, pat,
and kiss the you in me,
puzzled yet delighted by
that first shock of recognition.

I still hold that cute you inside,
as you unfold into youthful vanity,
gazing endlessly at yourself
while primping, teasing, plucking
and dabbing *My Sin*

behind your ears and knees
and in your cleavage.
I see you slide into silk and lace
beneath your wine-red velvet dress,
then painstakingly put on your face

over your face. I, alone, saw you later
lipstick smudged, mascara streaks,
the light gone out of your eyes.
Then in the morning, pale and green,
showering again and again, as if you were the slime.

So now you're past your prime,
I see your body shift;
the barnacle skin and bunions.
your face wrinkled and creased,
your eyes unadorned and wise.

Now, you are so beautiful.

Danielle Mitchell

Single Women's Rehabilitation Day

Think of me as light, imperishable. Think small,
think stubborn bean of a light on & ongoing toward
whatever, whatever is out there. An island,
or a morning. Maybe it's a boat; I don't know.
I am that light.

Today the doctor said if I go in the sun I'll get a rash.
She didn't say if that was the exposed skin or
if my whole body would be covered by daylight
& I didn't ask. For the first time in weeks
I wanted to go outside. Wanted to interrogate
my face with sun or cloud. Things are finally starting
to turn around, I thought. If we could all
repeat it like this: *I am*

imperfect, I am imperfect, I am imperfect but I know
how to dance. Let that be the journey's new slogan.
On the open range it will be harder to contain
my anxiety. I'll take fewer medicines. You will call me
a lark & my eyes will show their light at the seams.
We will cry into each other. We will circle the wagons
build the grandest campfire & let everything breathe.
We will make a day of it we'll call it Single Women's
Rehabilitation Day, call it that

& laugh as if all I need is a man. I tell you I am a light.
Come to me on the river; we'll shove ourselves into
the water's smoky path. Whenever you're drowning,
remember—let someone down, let someone down
so hard you come back up more yourself. That rarity.
That luminosity. That is you, we sail to at night.

Rose Mary Neff

Perfection is a Flaw

Acknowledgments

Contributor Bios

Alexis Rhone Fancher's book of erotic poems, *How I Lost My Virginity To Michael Cohen and Other Heart Stab Poems* (Sybaritic Press, 2014) is available online. She's been published in *RATTLE, Slipstream, Chiron Review, Ragazine* and elsewhere. Her photos are published worldwide. Alexis is poetry editor of *Cultural Weekly*. www.alexisrhonefancher.com

Alice Kociemba is the author of *Bourne Bridge* (forthcoming by Turning Point) and the chapbook, *Death of Teaticket Hardware*. She is the 2015 Guest Editor of Common Threads, the poetry discussion project of Mass Poetry. She directs *Calliope Poetry Series* at the West Falmouth Library in Massachusetts. www.calliopepoetryseries.com

Alison Stone wrote *Dangerous Enough, Borrowed Logic, From the Fool to the World,* and *They Sing at Midnight,* which won the 2003 Many Mountains Moving Award. She was awarded *Poetry*'s Frederick Bock Prize and *New York Quarterly*'s Madeline Sadin award. She created The Stone Tarot and is a psychotherapist.

Amanda Rochelle Martin is an unapologetic Feminist killjoy and artist from the Inland Empire. She worships the moon and is perpetually in the process of unravelling her cocoon. Lucid Moose Lit is the first press to publish her work.

Amy Wright is the Nonfiction Editor of Zone 3 Press and *Zone 3* journal and the author of five chapbooks. Some of her published pieces are online at: http://www.awrightawright.com

Angelita Ortega was once called "GooGoo" (an embarrassing childhood nickname she hated) and "GooGoo-Lita" (only by her mama). In 2013, Angelita began showing her artwork as gooGHOULita, a tribute to her mother who passed away of breast cancer in 2010. gooGHOULita's artwork reflects her love of music, cult movies, beer and love.

Annie Freewriter discovered her ability and need to write in a memoir writing group. Her love for memoir started as a teen when she read every biography and autobiography on her library shelf. Now she's writing her own story and won't look back until she's done. Follow her at anniefreewriter.net.

Ashley M. Jones will receive her MFA in Poetry from Florida International University in May 2015. Her work appears or is forthcoming in *Night Owl, The Harvard Journal of African American Public Policy, pluck!, Valley Voices: New York School Edition, Fjords Review: Black American Edition* and *PMS poemmemoirstory*.

BC Petrakos is a storyteller, performance artist, playwright and Pushcart–nominated writer. Her dynamic, tell-it-all approach has won over audiences in California, Chicago, New York, London and Edin. She is widely published with three books, and is a founding member of International Word Bank Productions and CFO of Baxter Daniels Ink Press.

Beth Cooley's work has appeared in a number of journals and anthologies, and she has published two YA novels with Delacorte Press. She lives in Spokane, WA, and teaches writing and literature at Gonzaga University.

Beth McIlvaine stumbled into a spoken word tent at Lollapalooza when she was 13 and it changed her life. She has been published in *51%*, *The Valley of Contemporary Poets Anthology* and *Don't Blame the Ugly Mug: An Anthology*. She just finished her Ph.D. in Biostatistics from USC's Keck School of Medicine.

Carmel Reid Mawle is the founder of Writing for Peace and editor of *DoveTales Literary Journal*. Mawle's work appears in *Smokelong Quarterly Review*, *Contemporary World Literature* and *SPACES Literary Magazine*. Her Pushcart-nominated story, "The Calisia," appears in *KNOT Literary Magazine*, along with her interview of revolutionary poet, Sam Hamill.

Cat Dixon is the author of *Too Heavy to Carry* (Stephen F. Austin Press, 2014). Her work has appeared in numerous journals and anthologies including *Sugar House Review*, *Midwest Quarterly* and *Eclectica*. She teaches creative writing at the University of Nebraska, Omaha. Dixon is the board secretary of The Backwaters Press, a nonprofit publishing house in Omaha.

Charlotte San Juan, exiled to Shanghai, China, currently works for NYU Shanghai Public Affairs. When not writing articles or photographing university shenanigans, she haunts an awe-inspiring hole-in-the-wall dumpling joint and thinks about what her cat is doing in California. All of this she does like a girl.

Hello, my name is Chelsea Krob. The work that I make is my way of starting a conversation with the viewer about how I have perceived our society by looking up close at the individual as well as our collective identity as a society.

Christina Foskey is a Californian mommy-to-be, expecting a GIRL, whose work has appeared in such places as: *The San Gabriel Valley Quarterly*, *Cadence Collective*, *The East Jasmine Review*, *Shark Reef*, *Gutters and Alleyways: Perspectives on Poverty and Struggle* and more. She was recently awarded 3rd place by the annual *Lummox* anthology in poetry.

Christina Elaine Vasquez is a poet, storyteller, visual and performance artist from Long Beach, California. She has been published in *The Holy Automatic*, and her collages featured in *BETEP #1*. She creates events under the moniker, Shezilla, and is often found at the local bar swaying slowly to the beat.

Christine Brandel is a writer and photographer. She published *Tell This To Girls: The Panic Annie Poems* in 2013. She is a PopMatters columnist and rights the world's wrongs via her character Agatha Whitt-Wellington at Everyone Needs An Algonquin. More of her work can be found at clbwrites.com.

Claire Ibarra's photographs have appeared in numerous journals, magazines and anthologies, including *Roadside Fiction, SmokeLong Quarterly, Alimentum~The*

Literature of Food, Foliate Oak and *Blue Fifth Review.* She was an artist in residence for *Counterexample Poetics* and is currently art director for *Gulf Stream Magazine.*

Clifton Snider is the internationally celebrated author of ten books of poetry, including *Moonman: New and Selected Poems* (2012), and four novels: *Loud Whisper, Bare Roots, Wrestling with Angels: A Tale of Two Brothers* and *The Plymouth Papers* (2014). He has published hundreds of poems, fiction, reviews and articles internationally.

Dana Anastasia lives and writes in Washington State, west of the Cascade Mountains. Her work has been published in *Extract(s), InkSpeak, Enigma Rag* and the Aborted Society zine. Her first chapbook, *Songs From the Hollow Alder,* was released in 2013 by the Black Dog Arts Coalition.

Daniel McGinn has been active in the Long Beach Poetry Scene for over 20 years. His poetry has appeared in numerous publications and he recently received an MFA in writing from Vermont College of Fine Arts. His most recent book of poems, *1000 Black Umbrellas,* was published by Write Bloody.

Danielle Mitchell has received the Editor's Choice Award from *The Mas Tequila Review.* Recent work appears in *Harpur Palate, H_NGM_N* and *Bellevue Literary Review.* She is an alumna of the Squaw Valley Community of Writers and poetry editor at *Wherewithal.* Danielle lives in Long Beach where she directs The Poetry Lab.

Daryna Barykina, born in Kyiv, Ukraine, graduated from the Kyiv School of Photography in 2010. She concurrently completed her master's degree in Business Administration at WIUU, Ukrainian-American Liberal Arts Institute Wisconsin International University (USA). She now resides in Florida, where she started her career as a beauty and fashion photographer.

Debbie J Cho is a photographer and visual artist currently based in Los Angeles. www.debbiejcho.com

Deirdre (Didi) Favreau, artist and musician, is currently living way far up in northern California...Yreka. Photography is one of her best mediums. See more photographic images at http://www.harngallery.com. Her latest music CD, *DEAL WITH IT,* can be heard at http://www.cdbaby.com/Artist/DidiFavreau.

Denise R. Weuve is a Pushcart Prize Nominee whose work has appeared in *San Pedro River Review, HEArt Journal, South Coast Poetry Journal, Four Chambers* and several other journals. She is founder and head editor of *Wherewithal,* and is poetry editor for *Cease, Cows!* Currently, she is earning an MFA from Queens University of Charlotte.

Don Kingfisher Campbell's poetry has recently been published in the anthologies *Poems To F*ck To, San Pedro River Review, Attack of the Poems, Gutters & Alleyways* and *Lummox #3;* and in cyberspace on the *Writer's Ezine, One Sentence Poems, Cadence Collective, Camel Saloon, Verse-Virtual, Tower Journal* and *Oddball Magazine* websites.

Donna Hilbert's latest book is *The Congress of Luminous Bodies,* from Aortic Books. *The Green Season* (World Parade Books), a collection of poetry and prose, is available in an expanded second edition. Her work is widely anthologized, most recently in *The Widows' Handbook*, Kent State University Press. More at www.donnahilbert.com

Dr. Ernest Williamson III has published work in over 550 journals. Williamson has published poetry in journals such as *The Oklahoma Review* and *The Copperfield Review*. His artwork has appeared in journals such as *The Columbia Review* and *The Tulane Review*. Dr. Williamson is an Assistant Professor of English at Allen University.

Elaine Mintzer has been published in a number of journals and anthologies including *Lummox, But Who's Counting, Israel Voices* and *13 Los Angeles Poets*. Elaine's first collection, *Natural Selections*, was published by Bombshelter Press in 2005. She writes and teaches writing in Los Angeles.

Elena Rodriguez was born in 1988 in Minnesota and raised in Florida. She attained her Bachelor of Fine Arts in Photography. She works in photography, time-based media, illustration and mixed media. Her focus is conceptual self-portraiture that explores identity, gender issues, space, and individuality. She is currently working in Jacksonville, Florida.

Elmast Kozloyan is a poet trapped in limbo between magic and reality (though seldom chooses the latter). At the age of fifteen she won silver for poetry in the Scholastic Art and Writing Awards and since then has been published in places such as *Cadence Collective, Pacific Review* and *Los Angeles Times*.

Erin Parker started out as an English major, fell in love with Art History, and ended up in art school studying commercial Interior Design. Erin is a 2014 Best of the Net Short Fiction Nominee. Her work has been published by *Drunk Monkeys, The Altar Collective, Lost in Thought, Red Fez* and several issues of *Uno Kudo*.

F. Douglas Brown is the author of *Zero to Three* (University of Georgia Press, 2014), and recipient of the 2013 Cave Canem Poetry Prize. His poems have appeared in numerous journals, and recently Mr. Brown was featured in *Poets and Writers Magazine* as one of their Debut Poets of 2014 (Jan/Feb 2015).

Fernando Gallegos is a Long Beach artist born and raised. He is heavily inspired by the human form and always searching to evoke the feeling of movement and emotion. Find more info and keep updated at FB: Fernando.Gallegos.LBC and Instagram: @fgraphix

Frank Kearns was raised in New England. He is transformed into a Southern Californian by time in Venice, years at the Bethlehem Steel mill in Vernon, and a long career in the aerospace industry. He lives and writes with his wife Carol in Downey, California.

G. Murray Thomas has been an active part of the SoCal poetry scene for over 20 years. He currently edits a monthly listing of poetry events for Poetix.net, the source for information about SoCal poetry. He has published two books of poetry, *My Kidney Just Arrived* (Tebot Bach, 2011) and *Cows on the Freeway* (iUniverse, 1999).

Helen Yeoman is an LA-based poet and member of Writers at Work. She's fascinated by how femininity is projected through the various fitness and lifestyle magazines she has helped publish for nearly a decade. She looks forward to giving this anthology to her niece and nephew.

Jackie Joice is a writer, photographer, qualitative researcher and volunteer at the Point Fermin Lighthouse in San Pedro, CA.

Jaclyn Weber is a California native and recent graduate of Bradley University. A feminist writer, whose work has been published by: *The Feminist Wire, NonBinary Review, Pentimento Magazine* and Write Bloody Publishing. Jaclyn has also performed her slam poetry across the nation at numerous universities. To read more of her work visit: http://jaclynweber.com/

Jan Presley taught, writes...lives with her husband in Southern Illinois' Shawnee Hills. Her poem honors complex global issues of clitoridectomy and infibulation; Freud's fleeting statement sets additional possible contexts of sexual abuse, shame, disassociation—or the fact that clitoridectomy was and is performed in the western world, including USA.

Jennifer Jackson Berry is the author of the chapbooks *When I Was a Girl* (Sundress Publications) and *Nothing But Candy* (Liquid Paper Press). Her poems have appeared or are forthcoming in *Booth, The Emerson Review, Harpur Palate* and *Whiskey Island*, among others. She lives in Pittsburgh, Pennsylvania.

JL Martindale writes stuff. She does other stuff, too. That other stuff she does often influences the stuff JL Martindale writes. Her poetry has been published with *Cadence Collective,* Bank Heavy Press, *San Gabriel Valley Poetry Quarterly,* Lucid Moose Lit, *A Poet is a Poet* anthologies and more.

Joan Jobe Smith, founding editor of *PEARL* and *Bukowski Review,* CSULB & UCI MFA graduate, has been published internationally since 1974 in more than 1,000 literary journals. She is author of the literary profile *Charles Bukowski: Epic Glottis: His Art & His Women (& me),* 22 poetry collections and recently-published prose memoir *TALES OF AN ANCIENT GOGO GIRL.*

K. Andrew Turner writes literary and speculative fiction, poetry and nonfiction. He teaches and mentors creative writers near Los Angeles, where he lives, works and writes in the San Gabriel Valley. He is the Editor-in-Chief of *East Jasmine Review* and a freelance editor. You can find more at his website: www.kandrewturner.com

Karen Boissonneault-Gauthier is an internationally published visual artist, photographer, writer and poet. She has shot cover art for *Zen Dixie Magazine, Vine Leaves* and *Crack the Spine.* Karen has also been featured in *Artemis Journal, Cactus Heart Press, Synaesthesia Magazine, Dactyl* and *Fine Flu Literary Journal.* Follow Karen @KBG_Tweets.

Karen S. Córdova is a writer and business woman who lives in Irvine, CA. She has been featured in many poetry and *ekphrasis* events throughout the country. Her book, *Farolito,* will be published in Spring 2015 by 3: A Taos Press. This true story casts light on the dark subject of elder abuse, but also illuminates a jagged path to solution and unexpected healing.

Karie McNeley is a two-wheelin' creative writer and artist from Lakewood, CA. She can be spotted in the wilds of suburbia chatting it up with cats, harboring a family of turtles and riding her bike through town in search of things unknown. Every speck tells a story.

Karla Cordero is a Loft Literary Spoken Word Immersion Fellow and Editor of *Spit Journal*. Her poetry is published in *Word Riot, The Acentos Review* and elsewhere. Her first chapbook, *Grasshoppers Before Gods*, is to be published in 2015 by Dancing Girl Press. You can follow her work at www.spitjournal.com.

Kathryn Pellman has a Certificate in Fashion Design and has been sewing since she could thread a needle. Her whimsical quilts celebrate and explore women and femininity. Fashion and quilting are combined to create single frame cartoon stories starring long limbed and knobby kneed fashionistas that invoke fashion illustration.

Keayva Mitchell is a twenty-two-year-old poet currently living in Long Beach, California. Some of her favorite poets include Terrance Hayes, Cristin O'Keefe-Aptowicz and Rachel McKibbens. Keayva has slowly and awkwardly embedded herself in the Long Beach poetry/music/art scene and has no plans to leave it any time soon.

Kelsey Bryan-Zwick is a recent Pushcart Prize Nominee, a bookbinder and an artist. Find her poems in *A Poet Is A Poet, No Matter How Tall*, at *Cadence Collective*, in *East Jasmine Review*, and at *The Camel Saloon*. Kelsey's second chapbook, *Watermarked*, is now out by Sadie Girl Press.

Kim Dower has two collections of poetry, *Air Kissing on Mars* and *Slice of Moon*, both out from Red Hen Press with a third, *Last Train to the Missing Planet* coming in spring of 2016. Kim's work has appeared in Garrison Keillor's "The Writer's Almanac," *Ploughshares, Barrow Street, Rattle* and *Eclipse*. www.kimdowerpoetry.com

Kirsten Clodfelter is a freelance writer living in the Midwest. She is the author of *Casualties* (RopeWalk Press, 2013), a chapbook of homefront and war stories, and her work has been published in *Salon, xoJane, The Good Men Project, The Iowa Review, Narrative Magazine, Green Mountains Review* and *Brevity*, among others. She blogs at WTFMommying.com.

Kristina Shue is an eccentric secular agnostic earth-based spiritualist, writer and all-around creative type currently living in Ohio where she is trying to figure out what adulthood means for someone whose regrets have left them as of yet degree-less. She will eventually finish her bachelor's in Writing (maybe).

LeAnne Hunt lives with her daughter and an overly sassy cat. She is a regular at the Ugly Mug reading in Orange and at the Poetry Lab workshop in Long Beach. She was published in *LUMMOX Three, Gutters & Alleyways: Perspectives on Poverty and Struggle* and *Cadence Collective* (cadencecollective.net/poets/leanne-hunt/).

Lee Kottner lives in New York City, and is a writer, editor, educator and agitator. Her poetry has appeared in several literary journals and small press anthologies and in a chapbook from Blue Stone Press. She teaches at New Jersey City University and the City University of New York.

Leigh Anne Hornfeldt is the author of two poetry chapbooks and is the editor of Two of Cups Press. In 2012 she received the Kudzu Prize in Poetry.

Lori McGinn is a elegant homemaker, expert cookie baker and a highly gifted illustrator who can spit out a poem now and again. Her chapbook, *Waiting*, is a part of the Laguna Poets Series.

Mara Buck writes, paints and rants in a self-constructed hideaway in the Maine woods. Awarded/short-listed by Faulkner/Wisdom, Hackney Awards, with work in *Drunken Boat*, *HuffPost*, *Crack the Spine*, *Blue Fifth*, *Writing Raw*, *Pithead Chapel*, *Apocrypha*, *Tishman Review*, *Stepping Stones*, *Linnet's Wings*, plus anthologies. A novel is forthcoming.

Mark A. Fisher is a writer, poet and playwright living in Tehachapi, CA. His column "Lost in the Stars" appears in Tehachapi's *The Loop* newspaper. His plays have appeared on stages around California. His poetry has appeared in *Lummox, The San Gabriel Valley Poetry Quarterly* and *Gutters and Alleyways*.

Mary Torregrossa is an Adult School ESL teacher. The Arroyo Arts Collective featured Mary in the 2014 "Poetry In The Windows." Her poem "Signs" was published in Juan Felipe Herrera's *Poems for Unity*. Poems also appear in the Pacific Coast Poetry Series: Poets of Los Angeles.

Meg Eden's work has been published in various magazines, including *Rattle, Drunken Boat, Eleven Eleven* and *Gargoyle*. Her poem "Rumiko" won the 2015 Ian MacMillan award for poetry, and she has four poetry chapbooks in print. She teaches at the University of Maryland. Check out her work at: www.megedenbooks.com

Melissa Dale is a photographer & filmmaker with an emphasis in creative portraiture. She is currently shooting a series of photographs using the medium she started on, 35mm film! Her lifestyle is a bit nomadic, but California will always be her home base. You can find more work online at melissadale.net.

Melissa Grossman is a member of Paradigm Poets in Los Angeles, CA. She has been published in *Kansas City Voices, Common Ground Review, In the Company of Women, Askew, Quintessence, Windows* and *Gutters & Alleyways: Perspectives on Poverty and Struggle*. Melissa is a stained glass artist, living in Simi Valley with her golden retriever, Molly.

Michael Cantin is aspiring poet and sloth fanatic residing somewhere in the wilds of Orange County, California, writing fitfully between bouts of madness and periods of lucid concern. You can find his work in *The East Jasmine Review, Hobo Pancakes, 50 Haiku*, several anthologies, and elsewhere.

Peggy Dobreer is a recent Pushcart Nominee for *Cadence Collective* anthology. Her first collection, *In The Lake of Your Bones*, was released by Moon Tide Press in March 2012. She hosts THE RwlrGiHtTe READ and teaches E=Mc2BODIED POETRY WORKSHOPS. www.peggydobreer.com

Raquel Reyes-Lopez is a Gemini born in the year 1994. Her debut chapbook, *Born to Electrify*, was recently published with Sadie Girl Press. She has had her poetry published with *Cadence Collective, Poetry in Motion, East Jasmine Review* and other literary journals. You can follow her blog at contactraquel.wordpress.com

Raundi Moore-Kondo is a writer, poet, publisher, singer/songwriter, writing coach and founder of For The Love Of Words Creative Writing Workshops & Small Press. When Raundi isn't pushing poetry on people she is bassist and singer for the bands Hurt and the Heartbeat and Daisy UnChained. www.theloveofwords.com

Ricki Mandeville's work has appeared in *Comstock Review, San Pedro River Review, Spot Lit, Pea River Journal* and other publications. A freelance editor in Huntington Beach, CA, she is the author of *A Thin Strand of Lights* and is working on her second book.

Robin Steere Axworthy is a native Californian who lived many places before returning home in 1983. She has been writing since childhood in the interstices among growing up, marriage, child rearing, teaching, dancing, reading, etc. She is currently writing poetry and working on two novellas.

Roy Anthony Shabla is a poet and painter living in the Los Angeles area. He currently has nine books of poetry in print. He is Director of Collections for Downey Museum of Art and sits on the advisory board of Nuvein Foundation for Literature and the Arts. He hosts a monthly gathering for artists, poets, musicians and other creative people called The Green Salon.

Sabrina Fedel has worked as an environmental lawyer, writer and teacher. Sabrina is a 2014 graduate of Lesley University's MFA in Creative Writing program, with a concentration on Writing for Young People. You can learn more about her at www.sabrinafedel.com, where she blogs about writing, learning disabilities and life.

Sandra Ramos O'Briant is the author of *The Sandoval Sisters' Secret of Old Blood* (La Gente Press, 2012). The novel won first place in two categories at the 15th annual ILBA, 2013: Best Historical Fiction and Best First Novel. Her short stories and creative nonfiction have appeared in numerous print and online journals. www.sramosobriant. com

Sarah ChristianScher is a poet trapped in a scientist's body. When not at the Ugly Mug, Sarah is harassing sea slugs at Cal Poly Pomona. Recent work has been published by Silver Birch Press. The poem in this anthology is dedicated to Grandma Esther, Nonnie, Amanda Cary and Diane Cary.

Sarah Lilius lives in Arlington, VA, where she's a poet and an assistant editor at ELJ Publications. Her work can be found in various journals including *Stirring, the Denver Quarterly* and *The Lake*. She is the author of *What Becomes Within* (ELJ Publications, 2014). Her website is sarahlilius.com.

Sarah Wheatley lives on the wet side of the Cascades and loves home, mountains, plants, dirt, bikes, backpacking, farming, food, working outside, community, old folk songs and books. When traveling, she is most delighted and at ease when she is invited into someone's kitchen.

Sharon Elliott is from Seattle, living in Oakland and has been featured in poetry readings in the Bay Area. Four years in the Peace Corps in Latin America laid the foundation for her activism in multicultural women's issues. She is an initiated Lukumi priest of Scot/Sámi/African Carribbean ancestry.

Shelia Cooper received her B.A. in English from UNC Greensboro and her M.A. in English and African American Literature from NC A&T State University. She is currently working on her M.F.A. in poetry at Queens University of Charlotte. She lives with her husband and daughter in Burlington, NC.

Susan Lefler's poems have appeared in a number of journals and anthologies. Her first book *Rendering the Bones* (Wind, 2011) won honorable mention in the 2012 Oscar Arnold Young Contest. She lives in Brevard, NC, and is studying for an MFA in poetry at Queens University, Charlotte, NC.

Susana H. Case's newest book is *4 Rms w Vu* (Mayapple Press). Author of four full-length poetry collections and four chapbooks, including *The Scottish Café*, re-released in a Polish-English version, *Kawiarnia Szkocka*, by Opole University Press, she is a Professor at the New York Institute of Technology. http://iris.nyit.edu/~shcase/.

Tamara Madison is the author of the collection *Wild Domestic* (Pearl Editions, July 2011) and the chapbook *The Belly Remembers* (Pearl Editions, 2004). Tamara is a California native who grew up on a citrus farm in the Coachella Valley. She teaches French and English in a high school in Los Angeles.

Woman in the Raw is a project conceived by photographer Tari Gunstone and all-around earth savvy wild woman Bailey Kelly Burger (pictured) to celebrate natural femininity and bring awareness to the healing tools women have. Check out the project and join in on the conversation: womanintheraw.tumblr.com

Taylor Wilson, born January 10, 1995, works predominantly in the medium of photography but also includes painting, drawing and some ceramics.

Terry Wolverton has authored ten books of poetry, fiction and creative nonfiction, including *EMBERS* and *INSURGENT MUSE*. Former Director of the Woman's Building, she's the founder of Writers At Work, a creative writing studio, and Affiliate Faculty in the MFA Writing Program at Antioch University Los Angeles. www.terrywolverton.com

Tobi Alfier is a five-time Pushcart Nominee and a Best of the Net Nominee. Her current chapbook, *Romance and Rust,* is from Blue Horse Press. Her collaborative full-length collection, *The Color of Forgiveness*, is available from Mojave River Press. She is the co-editor of San Pedro River Review (www.sprreview.com).

Toti O'Brien is an artist, writer and perfomer, also know as the Italian Accordionist with an Irish last name. You can learn more about her work at totihan.net

Trista Dominqu was born and raised in Southern California. She contributes much of her work to her memories. She believes she learned to form poems from sitting for long hours in a rocking chair listening to her grandmother's stories. She is married with three children. Her first chapbook, *Beauty of Muttliness,* is available online.

Viannah E. Duncan hails from the Los Angeles area and writes nonfiction by compulsion, poetry by inspiration, and reviews when the mood strikes. An editor by trade, she holds a Master of Fine Arts in creative writing and has been published in several small literary journals and anthologies. For more, visit her online at www.duncanheights.com.

Yvonne M. Estrada is a poet and photographer. Her recent chapbook, *My Name On Top of Yours,* features a crown of sonnets and original photographs about graffiti in Los Angeles. Her poetry has been published in *Mischief, Caprice & Other Poetic Strategies, Pulse Magazine, Verse Wisconsin* and *Talking Writing.*

Previously Published

Grateful acknowledgment is made to the editors of the following publications, in which some version of these works originally appeared.

Downer Magazine: "Under Water"
First of the Month: "Haunting"
Still Journal: "Dusting"
The Round Table: "The Little Little Little Little Little Little Dream"
Night Owl: "spin•ster"
Valley Voices: "What It Means To Say Sally Hemings"
Eighty Degrees and Thunder: "The One With Untamed Hair"
Spry Literary Journal: "A Wife Is A Hope Chest"
Counterexample Poetics: "Arrival"
Moonman: New and Selected Poems: "La Reina de Taos Pride & Pueblo"
Cadence Collective: "Interview with Sister [Age 44]," "Single Women's Rehabilitation Day"
Deep Red: "Vocabulary Builders"
Transforming Matter: "The Swimmer"
Natural Selections: "Stigma"
Los Angeles Times: "The first and possibly last poem I will ever write on this matter"
Cows on the Freeway: "Give Me Real Boobs"
When I Was a Girl: "When I Was a Girl"
PEARL: "What I Learned from the Movies"
Rattle Magazine: "Boob Job"
As It Ought to Be: "Because Misogyny"
The Intimacy Archive: "Poem for T"
The Lake Literary Magazine: "No Way...," "Memory Machine"
Rotary Phones: "Schürze"
In The Lake of Your Bones: "Color Me Gray"
Born to Electrify: "Scraped"
Destination Providence: "Play Like a Girl"
Viva La Feminista: "Crispy Feminist Flan Cake:"
Chiron Review: "The Divorce"
Stirring: "What I Mean When I Say Cartwheel"
sky poems: "rain poem"
Alyss: "War for Dinner"
Atticus Review: "Pack Animals"
East Jasmine Review: "Unknown Employee"
Our End Has Brought the Spring: "Games"
Expectations: "Everywhere," "Split," "Strip"
She Did It Anyway: "Ratatattoos"
Only: "Belladonna of the Night," "Belladonna of the Night," "Echoes of Mine"
Zero to Three: "Dear Defiance"

Thank You

Lucid Moose Lit is grateful to the following individuals and organizations for helping bring this book to life. We could not have done it without you!

A message from our Press Sponsor Mojave River Press & Review:

Mojave River Press and Review is proud to support Lucid Moose Lit social justice literary projects. We encourage you to do likewise, however possible—contribute writing, purchase anthologies, offer volunteer hours, make financial contributions; working together creates meaningful help for people in need. We also encourage you to check out both the brilliant Mojave River Press book catalog and our eclectic literary journal, the Mojave River Review. We feature award-winning authors in poetry, fiction, and non-fiction, right alongside exciting new voices. You can find it all, including social media links, at MojaveRiverPress.com. Let's work together for better.

Thank you to Tina Matuchniak who signed on as a BOOK SPONSOR for *Like a Girl*! You are a brilliant, inspiring woman, and we appreciate you.

Thank you to WE Labs for letting us use the conference room for official Moose business! Many thanks to Raquel Reyes-Lopez, Keayva Mitchell, Jackie Joice and JL Martindale for their insight during the early stage of the editorial process.

Nancy would like to thank Gary Reissman for his very generous continued support. Thank you Gary! Alex Hattick and Holly Carpenter, my gratitude is endless for everything we share: ideas, plans, feelings, doubts, triumphs. Your support and friendship mean the world to me. Alejandro Duarte, thank you for asking the hard questions and pushing the vision forward. Adam Duran, thank you with all my heart for your love and patience. A huge thanks to my parents for their encouragement. Sarah and Terry, millions of thanks for your hard work and dedication this project. And to all the women who paved the way.

From Terry: First of all, thank you to Nancy and Sarah for including me in this project! I appreciate your faith in me. The discussions we had about the vision for the book and the artists and writers who submitted work were educational, challenging, and above all, inspiring. A humble and deeply-felt thank you to all who submitted artwork, poetry and prose to this project, and for your continued support of Lucid Moose's vision of social justice-focused projects.

From Sarah: Thank you to Nancy and Terry for this experience. I have grown as an editor, a designer, a publisher, a poet, and as a woman. I am continually humbled by my community of ridiculously creative and endlessly generous friends. Whether our paths have overlapped for decades, years, or just a few months, I am indebted to all the women in my life who have left an impact on me.

About the Editors

Nancy Lynée Woo is a 2015 PEN Center USA Emerging Voices Fellow, and founding editor of Lucid Moose Lit. She graduated from UC Santa Cruz with a degree in sociology, and is currently working on a collection of poems about her mixed heritage, called *The Great Divide*. Often caught cavorting around Long Beach, CA, she can also be found at nancylyneewoo.com.

Sarah Thursday advocates for local poets and poetry events through a Long Beach-focused poetry website called CadenceCollective.net, co-hosts a monthly reading with one of her poetry heroes, G. Murray Thomas, and started Sadie Girl Press as a way to help publish local and emerging poets. Her first full-length poetry collection, *All the Tiny Anchors*, is available now. Find and follow her on SarahThursday.com, Facebook or Twitter.

Terry Ann Wright recently received her master's degree from Goddard College, a progressive school that emphasizes community activism and democratic education. She has written and published poetry exclusively for the last fifteen years, receiving two nominations for the Pushcart Prize in the process. She spends her days ridding the world of comma splices, and nights planning food-based road trips and sometimes writing.

About the Cover Artist

Born and raised in Southern California, Rose Mary Neff is a self-taught artist inspired by the people and world around her. "I believe that I am connected to everything positive when I paint. My desire is that we all feel that connection. I believe we are all both the artist and the artwork."

Medium: All images used, including "Perfection is a Flaw," are acrylic paintings on canvas.

Made in the USA
San Bernardino, CA
12 September 2015